# MONTEVERDI

*Sacred, Secular,*
*And Occasional*
*Music*

Other books by DENIS STEVENS:


*The Mulliner Book*
*Thomas Tomkins*
*The Pelican History of Music* (editor, with Alec Robertson)
*Tudor Church Music*
*Plainsong Hymns and Sequences*
*Grove's Dictionary of Music and Musicians*, vol. 10 (editor)
*A History of Song* (editor)

# MONTEVERDI
## *Sacred, Secular, and Occasional Music*

## *Denis Stevens*

RUTHERFORD • MADISON • TEANECK
FAIRLEIGH DICKINSON UNIVERSITY PRESS
LONDON: ASSOCIATED UNIVERSITY PRESSES

Associated University Presses, Inc.
Cranbury, New Jersey 08512

Associated University Presses
Magdalen House
136 - 148 Tooley Street
London SE1 2TT, England


Library of Congress Cataloging in Publication Data

Stevens, Denis William, 1922-
    Monteverdi: sacred, secular, and occasional music.

    Bibliography:  p.
    Includes index.
    1.  Monteverdi, Claudio, 1567-1643. Works.
ML410.M77S8             784'.092'4             76-731
    ISBN 0-8386-1937-1

PRINTED IN THE UNITED STATES OF AMERICA

for Yehudi and Diana

*Itaque sine Musica nulla disciplina potest esse perfecta; nihil enim est sine illa.*

Isidore of Seville

# Contents

Preface                                                    9

### I  SECULAR VOCAL MUSIC

1   Introduction                                          15
2   Dramatic Madrigals                                    18
3   Dialogues                                             21
4   Madrigals without Continuo                            26
5   Madrigals with Continuo                               36
6   Canzonette                                            44
7   Trios with Continuo                                   47
8   Duets                                                 53
9   Songs with Continuo                                   58

### II  RELIGIOUS MUSIC

10  Introduction                                          65
11  Masses                                                67
12  Vespers (B.V.M.)                                      73
13  Vespers (de Tempore et de Sanctis)                    82
14  Compline                                              94
15  Motets                                                98

### III MUSIC FOR THE STAGE

16  Introduction                       107
17  In Genere Rappresentativo          110
18  Ballets                            116
19  Intermezzi and Tornei              124
20  Operas                             130

    Selected Bibliography              139
    Index                              142

# Preface

Claudio Monteverdi was born in 1567 at Cremona, and died at Venice in 1643. His career was divided between two appointments: as a player of stringed instruments (and later director of the duke's private music for chapel and chamber) at the Mantuan court of the Gonzaga from 1589 until 1612, then as *maestro di cappella* at St. Mark's, Venice, from 1613 until 1643. His compositions generated considerable artistic and literary comment from the year 1600 onwards, but it was not until 1887 that a thorough biographical and critical study was published—not by an Italian, but by a young German musicologist who had familiarized himself with all the available music and documents at first hand. Emil Vogel's *Claudio Monteverdi: Leben, Wirken im Lichte der zeitgenössischen Kritik und Verzeichniss seiner im Druck erschienenen Werke,* which appeared in the third volume of the *Vierteljahrsschrift für Musikwissenschaft,* can still put many a subsequent effort to shame by reason of its breadth, depth, and accuracy. A translation, with a few minor corrections and updatings, would even now be of inestimable value.

But the fact remains that in Vogel's day a complete edition of the music was not available. It has therefore been my main intent and purpose, in presenting this brief critical study, to refer to modern sources—regardless of their merits or deficiencies—throughout the discussions, with a view to making everything as useful and practical as possible. Although there is insufficient space in which to analyze every work mentioned, or to recount the stories of the operas, it must surely be agreed that Monteverdi's music is well enough known nowadays to have made the kind of initial, perhaps even powerful impression that spurs on the listener to formulate his own analysis and assessment of the materials at hand. My contributions are rather in the nature of new viewpoints or unpublished research, and to this end I have organized the chapters and subsections in such a way as to escape (as indeed I hope) from the tyranny of chronological order. Unusually in a book of this type, as much space is devoted to lost works as to certain extant ones, which may result in a more sharply focused overall view of the composer's total oeuvre.

In conclusion, I wish to thank the staff of Associated University Presses for their expert and patient cooperation, and my wife for her assistance and encouragement while this book was being prepared for publication.

D. S.
*Santa Barbara, California, 1977*

# MONTEVERDI

*Sacred, Secular,
And Occasional
Music*

# I
# SECULAR VOCAL
# MUSIC

# 1

# *Introduction*

Monteverdi's secular vocal music, although mainly found in his nine books of madrigals, cannot properly be understood simply in terms of the madrigal, nor can it be accurately dated merely by referring to the year of publication. Some of the compositions are not madrigals at all, and some of the dates bear no relationship whatever to the time of first performance. Works of outstanding importance will therefore be discussed in a categorical, rather than chronological order, this latter appearing below for purely bibliographical reference. Entries in italics denote anthologies featuring the music of other composers besides Monteverdi.

| DATE | SHORT TITLE (compiler) | Dedicatee/*Contents* |
|------|------------------------|----------------------|
| 1583 | Madrigali spirituali[1] | Alessandro Fraganesco (Cremona) |
| 1584 | Canzonette a 3 | Pietro Ambrosini (Cremona) |
| 1587 | Madrigali a 5 (I) | Count Marco Verità (Verona)[2] |
| 1590 | Madrigali a 5 (II) | Iacomo Ricardi (Milan) |
| 1592 | Madrigali a 5 (III) | Vincenzo, Fourth Duke of Mantua |
| *1594* | *Canzonette a 3* [I] (Morsolino) | *four canzonette* |
| 1603 | Madrigali a 5 (IV) | Accademici Intrepidi (Ferrara) |
| 1605 | Madrigali a 5 (V) | Vincenzo, Fourth Duke of Mantua |
| *1605* | *Nuovi Fioretti Musicali* (Franzoni) | *one canzonetta* |
| 1607 | Scherzi musicali a 3 | Don Francesco Gonzaga (Mantua) |
| *1608* | *Madrigali a 4-7* (de Wert)[3] | *two madrigals* |
| 1614 | Madrigali a 5 & 7 (VI) | [no dedication] |
| 1619 | Madrigali a 1,2,3,4, & 6 (VII) | Caterina Medici Gonzaga (Mantua) |
| *1623* | *Lamento d'Arianna. . .*[4] | *three monodies* |
| *1624* | *Madrigali* (Anselmi) | *one duet; one trio* |
| *1624* | *Quarto Scherzo* (Milanuzzi) | *three monodies* |
| 1632 | Scherzi musicali a 1 & 2 | Pietro Capello (Capo d'Istria) |
| *1634* | *Arie de diversi* (Vincenti) | *two monodies* |
| 1638 | Madrigali a 2-8 (VIII) | Ferdinand III, Emperor (Vienna) |
| 1640 | Selva morale e spirituale | *five spiritual madrigals* |
| 1651 | Madrigali e canzonette a 2 & 3 (IX) | Gerolamo Orologio (Venice) |

1. Only the Bassus part is extant; facsimile in xvi (appendix). For an exhaustive study of the genre and the texts, see Elena Ferrari Barassi, "Il madrigale spirituale nel Cinquecento e la raccolta monteverdiana del 1583," *Claudio Monteverdi e il suo tempo* (Verona, 1969), p. 217.

2. Biographies of Monteverdi invariably refer to Marco Verità as a Cremonese nobleman. In fact he was an eminent citizen of Verona, and one of the principal members of the Accademia Filharmonica there. He appears as one of three interlocutors in Pietro Ponzio's *Dialogo. . .ove si tratta della Theorica e Prattica di Musica* (Parma, 1595), also as dedicatee of secular anthologies in 1588 (*Giardinetto de Madrigali e Canzonette*, by various composers), and in 1598 (Paolo Funghetti's *Capriccii e Madrigali*). One reason for Monteverdi's dedication was undoubtedly his interest in obtaining an appointment at Verona.

3. Discussed and listed in Carol MacClintock, "New Sources of Mantuan Music," *Journal of the A.M.S.* 22 (1969): 508.

4. Also printed in 1623 by M. Fei and R. Ruuli in their anthology *Il maggio fiorito*.

On the first appearance of a title, in the following pages, reference will be made in parentheses to the relevant volume and page of the Malipiero edition.[5]

This should not be confused with *Rosaio Fiorito,* a cantata said to have been written for the birth of a son to the Governor of Rovigo in 1629. The dubious nature of this claim is fully discussed by Vogel, *Claudio Monteverdi,* pp. 391-92.

5. In spite of its many imperfections it is the only complete collection of Monteverdi's music available at the time of writing.

# 2

# Dramatic Madrigals

The apparently contradictory term *dramatic madrigal* derives from a Renaissance stage tradition whereby musicians sang and played out of sight of the audience. The medium was that of the drama, and the mode of performance that of the madrigal. But polyphony, as a seamless tonal tapestry apt for abstract thought, could not easily project concrete ideas and forthright speech unless it were modified both in sound and substance. Composers therefore took to writing in a chordal style, which is sometimes referred to as "choral recitative" although "chordal recitative" might be a more appropriate description. Nevertheless, a departure from the chamber-music ideals of madrigalian performance might often have been dictated by the size of the theater or room in which the drama was given, extra voices and even instruments being added to help the sound across the audience.

Monteverdi must have had to deal with this problem

when he contributed, along with other composers, to the music for Guarini's play *Il Pastor Fido*, published in 1590. The premiere eventually took place in 1595 at Ferrara, where Monteverdi already had close contacts among the virtuoso musicians and academy members to whom he dedicated his Fourth Book. This, together with the Fifth, contains eight excerpts from the play,[1] and such is their homogeneity of style in regard to predominantly chordal declamation that they must surely have been heard in the performances at Ferrara (1595), Crema (1596), or Mantua, where an exceptionally lavish production with intermezzi was given in 1598. A treatise on dramatic poetry by Angelo Ingegneri draws attention to the need for a special musical style in comedies and pastorals, whose choruses should be sung "most simply and in such a way that they differ only a little from ordinary speech."[2]

These settings, in the order in which they would occur in the drama, may be listed as follows: Act I, Scene 1, *Quell' augellin che canta* (iv, 66); I,2, *Cruda Amarilli* (v,i); III,3 *Ch'io t'ami* (v, 39); III,3, *Ah dolente partita* (iv, 1); III,4, *O Mirtillo* (v,5); III,4, *[Deh, Mirtillo] anima mia* (iv, 26); III,6 *M' è più dolce* (v,56); IV,9, *Ecco Silvio* (v,14). Some of them are lengthy, with two, three, or even—in the case of *Ecco Silvio*—five sections clearly intended for consecutive performance. And in all of them the style is harmonic and vertical rather than contrapuntal, aiming for great economy in time. Even so, about 1,600 lines had to be cut in the Manuan perform-

1. He set *O primavera* (iii, 62), as a genuine madrigal, using a shortened text that was apparently well known before the first published edition of the pastoral. This same text, set by Luzzaschi for solo voice and continuo, was published in 1601 among the *Madrigali per cantare e sonare* (modern ed. by A. Cavicchi, Brescia, 1965). On the other hand, the five-part settings by de Wert and Schütz are based on the fuller version in the printed edition of *Il Pastor Fido*.
2. MacClintock, *Giaches de Wert* (Rome, 1966), p. 181.

ance, in spite of Monteverdi's relatively rapid declamation. This example from the third section of *Ch'io t'ami* illustrates Mirtillo's anger at Amarilli's stony silence: "If you've nothing else to say, at least tell me to die, and you'll see me die!"

Ex. 1

# 3
# *Dialogues*

Monteverdi's secular dialogues, rarely discussed as a separate aspect of his madrigalian production, genuinely deserve detailed consideration since they form part of a continuing tradition of musical conversations whose remote origins go back to the Middle Ages.[1] A double-choir arrangement was frequently used for the many question-and-answer poems set to music in the sixteenth century. But it was not the only method: voices in duo or trio formation could be isolated within a polyphonic complex, and often with excellent results. This happens in *Io mi son giovinetta* (iv,59), which begins with a "Ferrarese" trio of high voices as the girl introduces herself. After a five-part interlude, the three lower voices represent the man's viewpoint.

1. The best general study of dialogues in music is Theodor Kroyer, "Dialog und Echo in der alten Chormusik," *Jahrbuch der Musikbibliothek Peters* 16 (1909): 13. More recent articles include those of Don Harrán, "Towards a Definition of the Early Secular Dialogue," *Music and Letters* 51 (1970): 37, and Denis Stevens, "Renaissance Dialogue Techniques," *Studies in Honor of Charles Warren Fox* (in progress).

The real dialogues begin with Book V, among the madrigals with compulsory continuo. *Ahi, come a un vago sol* (v,62) highlights two tenors, who might have been placed at some distance from the answering trios and quintets. The interplay is more subtle in *Troppo ben può questo tiranno Amore* (v, 71), where the soloist is a soprano, her shadows a trio or quartet. The lower voices gently stress the prelude to direct speech, joining in the dialogue as soon as it is launched: "Foolish heart, don't wait for him to do it." (Ex. 2)

*T'amo, mia vita* (v,90) is another miniature showpiece

Ex. 2

for soprano, based on a poem by Guarini, as were the previous dialogues. This musical declaration of love, probably written about the year 1600, may have been given its first performance by the court singer Claudia Cattaneo, who became Monteverdi's wife in 1599. *E così poco a poco tornò farfallo*[2] (v, 96) is Monteverdi's earliest surviving six-part madrigal. If the basic dialogue contrasts a duetting soprano and tenor against a male voice trio, there is sometimes a return to the older technique of Willaert and Andrea Gabrieli, who would "borrow" voices in order to make a duet into a trio, or a trio into a quartet. The holding back of the sixth voice — a kind of filler — until the peroration is a typical device of Monteverdi's, to be found in other types and textures.

*Questi vaghi concenti* (v, 104) ranks as a nine-part dialogue, but begins with an evenly balanced SATB/SATB section after the introductory sinfonia. This is a genuine classical dialogue, to which the new element of solo voices can be added thanks to the presence of the continuo instruments. When the second soprano joins in at last, the five-part choir could be doubled by the matching instrumental ensemble, all nine voices punctuating her soliloquy with reiterated chords to a sympathetic "Deh!"

Book VI contains three splendid dialogues. *A Dio, Florida bella* (vi, 38) reduces the conversation to that of a boy and a girl (tenor and soprano) balancing their delicately ornamented solos against descriptive passages sung by all five voices. This sonnet is by Giambattista Marini, but we do not know who wrote *Misero Alceo*

---

2. The unusual incipit is explained by the fact that this poem by Guarini is the third part of a literary triptych (pp. 102-4 in vol. 2 of the collected edition published at Verona in 1737), of which Monteverdi set the first — *Ahi, come a un vago sol* — and third, while Marenzio set the second (*Oimè, l'antica fiamma*). Certain lines and phrases recur in all three poems, demonstrating their interrelationship.

(v,91), about a shepherd whose sorry plight is already evident in the incipit. After the chorus has set the scene, Alceo sings of his sadness at leaving home and his girl friend (Lidia), whom he addresses in a kind of strophic song over a meltingly chromatic bass. This variation technique is of a loose kind, in which the three successive statements support first two, then four, then three lines of the poem.

Ex. 3

*Presso un fiume tranquillo* (v,113) draws on a poem of Marini featuring two lovers and a five-part chorus. The seven-voice tutti is heard only at the very end, where it repeats and fills out the music of the final duet, adding a tender and osculatory coda of its own. Dialogues are also found in the Seventh and Eighth Books *(Tirsi e Clori;*

*Lamento della Ninfa*), but they will be dealt with in the chapter on stage music since they belong to the *genere rappresentativo*. The last one of all, *Bel pastor* (ix,1) appeared in print after Monteverdi's death. It is a setting of a poem by his Florentine friend, Rinuccini — a charming piece of bucolic badinage whose every shade of cajolery and flattery is reflected in the changing moods and meters of the music.

# 4

# *Madrigals without Continuo*

Monteverdi's position astride the territores of the *prima e seconda prattica* is seen nowhere so clearly as in his madrigalian output. The four earliest books concentrate on the classical five-part unaccompanied madrigal, while the last three (and the *Selva morale*, which contains five compositions with Italian text) cleave to the continuo. In between them, Books V and VI offer madrigals in both styles, accompanied and unaccompanied, so that the total impression is one of symmetry and design though it must surely have been a historical accident.

| Unaccompanied madrigals | With and without B.C. | With Basso Continuo |
|---|---|---|
| Books I,II,III,IV | Books V & VI | Books VII,VIII,IX, & *Selva* |

The early madrigals of Book I show a remarkable grasp

of expressive harmony, telling effects of color, and a shrewd sense of form. *Ch'io ami la vita mia* (i,1) puns innocently upon the name of his patron, Verità, who must surely have approved of the suspended diminished fourths on such key words as *mora, afflitto, and morte*. Monteverdi was quick to guage the madrigalian possibilities of Guarini's *Baci soavi e cari* (i,14), already set by the Veronese composer Masnelli in 1585, and later to inspire Gesualdo and Girolamo Belli. In *Filli cara e amata* (i,21) Alberto Parma's harmlessly erotic poem generates music of quite exceptional beauty and subtlety. In the opening paragraph, the counterpoint pervades the thought as well as the music when the lover asks his girl: "That pretty mouth of yours—is it not mine?" (See Ex. 4)

*Fumia la pastorella* (i,27) is a miniature triptych, a set of three madrigals of which the central one is a May song by the shepherdess herself, and could perhaps be performed as a solo accompanied by instruments.[1] Another group might be formed by Guarini's *Ardo sì, ma non t'amo* (i,61) with the reply and counter-reply of his friend Tasso.[2]

In Book II Monterverdi shows an increasing awareness of the importance of choosing good poetry. He offers skilled settings of lyrics by Girolamo Casoni, Ercole Bentivoglio, Filippo Alberti, and Pietro Bembo, but the name that towers loftily above the others is that of Torquato Tasso, nine of whose poems spurred him toward new heights. The double madrigal that opens the book, *Non si levava ancor* (ii,1) displays an imaginative fusion of counterpoint and color, both helping to

---

1. The poem, by Antonio Allegretti, was first published in Atanagi's *Rime* of 1565 and appears as early as 1582 in a setting by Pietro Bianco as a canzona for a wedding.
2. Guarini's poem inspired Giulio Gigli to collect 28 different settings (including one by Monteverdi's teacher Ingegneri), published in 1585 as *Sdegnosi ardori*.

Ex. 4

S: Fil - li ca - ra ea - ma - ta, Dim - mi per cor - te -

A: Fil - li ca - rae a - ma - ta, Dim - mi per cor - te -

T: Fil - li ca - rae a - ma - ta, Dim - mi per cor - te -

T:

S: si - a, Ques - ta tua bel - la boc - ca, ques - ta tua bel - la boc - ca,

A: si - a, Ques - ta tua bel - la boc - ca, ques - ta tua bel - la boc - ca,

T: si - a, ques - ta tua bel - la boc - ca,

T: Non è mi - a?

S: non è mi - a, non è mi - a?

A: ques - ta tua bel - la boc - ca, non è mi - a?

T: non è mi - a, non è mi - a?

T: ques - ta tua bel - la boc - ca, non è mi - a?

heighten the contrast between the descriptions of the first
madrigal and the dialogue of the second. Another Tasso
setting that has achieved well-deserved fame is the match-
less dawn song, *Ecco mormorar l'onde* (ii,68). *Crudel,
perche mi fuggi?* (ii,83) often wrongly ascribed to Tasso is
actually by Guarini.[3] The point of the poem's last line is
effectively thrust home by means of opposing duets, with
the two sopranos as one unit, and the tenor and bass as
another.

Ex. 5

Book III, which enjoyed no fewer than seven reprints,
draws heavily on Guarini's *Rime*. The admiration for *O
come gran martire* (iii, 8) among the circle of Mantuan
and Ferrarese composers is demonstrated by the sensitive
setting of Carlo Gesualdo[4] as well as by Monteverdi's
memorable version, and the other examples of artistic
collaboration between court poet and composer maintain
a high level of excellence. Outstanding for their dramatic
thought (though they were not meant to be acted) are the

---

3. The misattribution arose because the original begins *Lasso, perchè mi fuggi*. It was
twice translated for the delectation of English madrigal singers: first by Thomas
Watson (1590), later by Nicholas Yonge (1597).
4. Gesualdo's setting appears in his second book (1594), and was also available some
years earlier under a pseudonym. The poem set by Gastoldi (Book I, 1588) begins with
the same incipit but thereafter diverges.

two sets of three madrigals based on Tasso's
*Gerusalemme Liberata*. In *Vivrò fra i miei tormenti* (iii,
87) we hear of Tancred's shame and sorrow for the

slaying of Clorinda,[5] a deed that was to be portrayed in quite another kind of music some thirty years later in Monteverdi's career. Emotion of a different kind pervades the other group, beginning with *Vattene pur, crudel* (iii, 48) which depicts the bitter fury of Armida abandoned by Rinaldo.[6] The composer's sensitivity to the poet's punctuation is such that he ends the first madrigal on a half-close so that the second can begin without pause, the reason being that stanza 59 ends with a comma and the finite verb does not appear until stanza 60. He is also aware of dramatic tension, omitting the next two stanzas and passing directly to 63, when Armida faints only to recover to an anguished outpouring—"And do I love him still, and on this sand / Still unreveng'd, still mourn, still weeping stand?[7] (Ex. 6)

Book IV also proved its popularity with five ordinary reprints and two more by Phalèse, who included a continuo part in order to adjust the volume to the prevailing fashion of the time. Apart from the *Pastor Fido* settings,[8] six further lyrics of Guarini are included, one of the most remarkable being *A un giro sol de begl' occhi* (iv, 49). The madrigal follows closely the bipartite nature of the poem, in which a glance from the beloved's eyes introduces the laughter of breezes, stillness of the sea, a new light in the heavens. In the second part, the lover bemoans the day when his innamorata was born, for her cruelty will bring about his death. His certainty is confirmed by reiterated unisons breaking into poignant suspension-chains:

5. Canto XII, 77-79.
6. Canto XVI, 59, 60, 63.
7. From the translation by Edward Fairfax, published in 1600 as *Godfrey of Bulloigne', or the Recoverie of Jerusalem.*
8. See chap. 2.

Ex. 7

There is some undeniably genuine "eye-music" at the beginning of *Luci serene e chiare* (iv, 35), where the two whole notes for the syllables "lu-ci" do indeed resemble a pair of eyes. The poem, by Ridolfo Arlotti, was set by Gesualdo in his fourth book (1596).[9] In the passionately expressive setting of Rinuccini's *Sfogava con le stelle* (iv, 15), the singers are allowed to declaim, in steady speech-rhythm, various phrases and lines of the poem, as if it were a psalm in falsobordone. Maurizio Moro makes a solitary appearance with his sensuous, bittersweet *Sì, ch'io vorrei morire* (iv, 78), and even Tasso turns up unexpectedly with a passage from *Gerusalemme Conquistata* — the poignantly chromatic *Piagne e sospira* (iv, 96)[10]

Book V has been dealt with mainly under the headings of dramatic madrigals and dialogues, but it should be noted that notwithstanding this highly specialized

9. See Glenn Watkins, *Carlo Gesualdo* (London, 1973), p. 128, n. 38.
10. First identified as such by Nino Pirrotta, *Scelte poetiche di Monteverdi* (Rome, 1968), p. 21. This valuable monograph first appeared as two articles in *Nuova Rivista Musicale Italiana* 2 (1968).

content and the obligatory continuo for the last six items, the volume enjoyed an enthusiastic welcome and was reprinted eight times, with two editions in the year 1615 alone. The implication on the title page that continuo instruments could also be added to the first thirteen madrigals may be counted as evidence in favor of a larger group of musicians for performances of the *Pastor Fido* excerpts. The English composer Walter Porter, who studied with Monteverdi in Venice, copied out (and in some cases arranged for a reduced ensemble) representative works from this and other volumes.[11]

Book VI, like its predecessor, includes madrigals both with and without continuo, yet there is a subtle difference in performance practice. Whereas the ordinary madrigals in Book V could be performed with continuo, there is nothing in Book VI to say that the two laments or the two Petrarch settings might be so performed. They are in fact best suited to an unaccompanied group of soloists. Exceptionally, Monteverdi makes no dedicatory gesture, and in view of the content of the volume, which concentrates on laments, songs of farewell and death, or unrequited love, it is quite possible that he privately dedicated the music to the memory of his wife, Claudia, who died in 1607, and Caterina Martinelli (the young singer intended for the part of Ariadne), who died in 1608.

The plan of the volume, like that of Book VIII,[12] falls into two separate sections in perfect balance with each other:

---

11. London, British Library Add. Ms. 31,440. For other contemporaneous manuscript versions, see the probably incomplete set of partbooks at Christ Church, Oxford, Mss. 878-880. Detailed information is given by Pamela J. Willetts, "A Neglected Source of Monody and Madrigal," *Music and Letters* 43 (1962):329.
12. See chap. 5.

|  | Section 1 | Section 2 |
|---|---|---|
| *unaccompanied* | | |
| Laments | Lasciatemi morire | Incenerite spoglie |
| Petrarch sonnets | Zefiro | Ohimè |
| | | |
| *concertato* | | |
| Madrigals | Una donna; A Dio | Qui rise; Misero; Batto qui |
| | | |
| Dialogue | Presso un fiume tranquillo | |

Although published in 1614, many of these pieces go back as far as 1607, which was the probable date of composition for the Petrarch sonnets. In that year, Duke Vincenzo and his court spent part of the summer at Sampierdarena, near Genoa, and a letter of Monteverdi's mentions the composition of two sonnets, probably for unaccompanied voices.[13] The emotional gulf between the octave and sestet of *Zefiro torna* (vi, 22) is searingly sensed in the music, in which dissonances reach an almost unbearable intensity at the end. *Ohimè, il bel viso* (vi, 70) is no less moving, but offers a wider range of textures, such as the remarkable passage in full five-part harmony combined with two-part rhythm ("I too was yours" / "For these must I burn and in them feel relief"):

Ex. 8

13. Further details in Denis Stevens, "Monteverdi's Necklace," *The Musical Quarterly* 59 (1973):370.

According to Giovanni Battista Doni, Monteverdi wrote his madrigal version of *Lasciatemi morire* (vi, 1) at the request of a Venetian nobelman,[14] thus complying with the wishes of another instead of following the dictates of his own conscience. This rearrangement was probably completed in 1611, but many years were to elapse before the solo version finally appeared in 1623. Doni was right to point out the incongruity of a woman's lament being sung by a quintet of mixed voices,[15] but it remained a popular version for those with no access to a continuo instrument. There is happily no attempt, in *Lagrime d'Amante al Sepolcro dell'Amata* (vi, 46), to match the convoluted cleverness of Agnelli's sestina by some comparable tour de force in the music. Monteverdi is content with honest declamation, relying more upon chords than upon counterpoint, the overall effect being one of reverent solemnity.[16]

14. Possibly Giovanni Matteo Bembo, in whose mansion Abbott Angelo Grillo attended musical evenings prior to 1620. Monteverdi's *Lament of Apollo* was heard there in 1620, as he explains in a letter dated February 1. Giovanni Battista Doni's comment is found in his *Lyra Barberina* (Florence, 1763), 2: App. 98.
15. Doni, 2: App. 26.
16. It should be noted that the verse-form of the sestina is usually upset by reprints based on the musical text, Monteverdi having exercised some license in introducing certain phrases before others. The final couplets of the first and second stanzas need adjusting so that the six key words occur in their proper order.

# 5

# *Madrigals with Continuo*

Two madrigals, patterned after but improving upon the *airs de cour* that Monteverdi heard on his visit to nothern Europe in 1599, may well date from the late Mantuan period. They are *Dolcissimo uscignuolo* and *Chi vuol haver felice* (viii, 271 and 280), both of them successful in alternating solo statements and tutti confirmations, like a dialogue in a musical rather than a literary sense.[1] They were not published until 1638, when Guarini's lyrics were already things of the past. *Una donna fra l'altre* (vi, 29) was delayed for only a few years, appearing first in 1609 as a sacred contrafactum[2] and then as a madrigal in 1614. The poetry of Giambattista Marini first exerted its influence on Monteverdi's madrigals in Book VI, where

---

1. The paired nature of these madrigals is emphasized in their reappearance, with Latin words, in the *Confitebor III* of the *Selva morale*. See chap. 13.
2. In Coppini's *Terzo Libro della musica di Claudio Monteverdi. . .fatta spirituale*, where its title is given as *Una es*.

the scintillating wordplay of a sonnet such as *Qui rise, O Tirsi* (vi, 77) clearly inspired musical ideas of comparable brilliance. No hint or allusion is missed by the ever-observant composer—the girl's laughing eyes prompt the sopranos, then the tenors, to indulge in fanciful flights of ornamented melody; the shepherd's pipes play in mellifluous thirds; the three graces reside in a trio of women's voices; arms locked in affection squeeze out strings of syncopated suspension. Every image is faithfully reflected in the score.

*A quest' olmo* (vii, 14), also based on a sonnet by Marini, was probably written for a soirée given by a Bembo, a Guistiniani, or a Mocenigo, in whose spacious palazzi the Venetian madrigal had developed in stature and instrumentation. This example, for six voices, with a pair each of violins and flutes, ranks as a worthy fore-runner of the later settings of Petrarch and Marini published in Book VIII (1638). The other madrigals of Book VII incline to a simpler but none the less expressive type, such as Tasso's *Al lume delle stelle* (vii, 129). *Amor, che deggio far* (vii, 182) is really a canzonetta, complete with ritornels for two violins and continuo.

There is ample evidence that Monteverdi, in his artistic maturity, chose the sonnet as the most suitable poetic medium for his serious works. Between the years 1624 and 1639, he wrote six compositions for 5, 6, 7, or 8 voices, with two violins and continuo, based on sonnets by Petrarch, Marini, and certain capable but anonymous imitators of those poets. It is also known that in 1628 he composed music for the state visit of Ferdinando II, Grand Duke of Tuscany, the texts being a series of five sonnets—*I cinque fratelli*—by Giulio Strozzi.[3] Unlike many of his creative brethren, Monteverdi took pains to

3. The music does not survive, but the poems were printed by Deuchino (Venice, 1628).

avoid setting only the sestet of a sonnet,[4] and in only one instance did he restrict a composition to the octave — *Vago augelletto* (viii, 222) — in which the sense is complete as far as it goes. There are elements here of the *air de cour*, the dialogue (a seventh voice is held back until near the end), and the cantata, Petrarch's singing bird flying freely between soprano, bass, and tutti. (Ex.9)

The opening poem of Marini's *La Lira: parte prima* appears as the first of the amorous madrigals of Book VIII — *Altri canti di Marte* (viii, 181), and it was successfully imitated in another sonnet by an unknown Venetian versifier for use as the parallel opening of the warlike madrigals — *Altri canti d'Amor* (viii, 1). The correspondence of ideas and resources in the two halves of this great anthology may be clearly seen from the italicized features in the following comparison:

| MADRIGALI GUERRIERI | | MADRIGALI AMOROSI |
|---|---|---|
| *Altri canti* d'Amor | *a 6; str.* | *Altri canti* di Marte (Marini) |
| Hor che'l ciel (Petrarch) | *a 6; str.* | Vago augelletto (Petrarch) |
| Gira il nemico | *small group* | Mentre vaga Angioletta (Guarini) |
| Se vittorie si belle | *two tenors* | Ardo, e scoprir |
| Armato il cor | *two tenors* | O sia tranquillo il mar |
| Ogni amante (Rinuccini) | *two tenors & bass* | Ninfa che scalza il piede |
| Ardo avvampo | | Dolcissimo; Chi vuol haver (Guarini) |
| Combattimento (Tasso) | *theatrical* | Lamento della Ninfa (Rinuccini) |
| | | Perchè; Non partir; Su su su |
| *Ballo*: Movete *(Rinuccini)* | *theatrical* | *Ballo* delle Ingrate *(Rinuccini)* |

4. The number of sestets (deprived of their octaves) that were set to music in the sixteenth century misled Lodovico Frati into listing several madrigals as not being based on texts of Petrarch, when in fact they are perfectly genuine. See "Il Petrarca e la Musica," *Rivista Musicale Italiana* 31 (1924):59 (esp. pp. 65-66).

A scheme of this nature can hardly be accidental, especially when considered in the light of the unusually lengthy preface to the entire collection. *Altri canti d'Amor,* an occasional work celebrating the triumphs of the Emperor Ferdinand III (dedicatee of Book VIII), makes ample and effective use of the bellicose formulae perfected for the *Combattimento,* in its picturesque introduction of the proud and violent god of war.[5] (See Ex. 10, p. 41)

*Ardo, avvampo* (viii, 107) calls for eight voices, but not in double-choir formation, for the warlike tones of the beginning demand a massed and panic-stricken series of shouts for ladders, hammers, hatchets, and water, all to quench the fires of love. The source of the conflagration is a pair of beautiful eyes, which dominate the sestet and lead gradually to a calm and unexpected close. In some ways the most impressive of the group is *Hor che'l ciel e la terra* (viii, 39), reflecting with crystal clarity Petrarch's portrayal of the contrast between the stillness of night and the turbulence of the lover's soul. Harmonic felicities abound, stressing the anguish of lamentation ("piango"), the bittersweet pains of love (a simultaneous C and C# on "dolce"), and the wounding and healing of but one hand ("una man sola mi risana e punge"). But even these are surpassed by the boldness and breadth of the peroration, which points up the remoteness of salvation through love by having the voices begin in a close triad and then expand to the maximum extent of their compass. (See Ex. 11, pp. 42-43)

Although they were included among the *Selva morale,* a collection of liturgical compositions published in 1641, two further Petrarch settings are properly considered as

5. For a discussion of Book VIII, see Denis Stevens, "Madrigali Guerrieri, et Amorosi," *The Musical Quarterly* 53 (1967):161.

Ex. 10

spiritual madrigals. Not only do they function as a dedicatory gesture at the beginning of the *Selva morale*; they also call to mind Petrarch's own comparable intention, for *O ciechi, il tanto affaticar che giova?* (xv, 1) comes from the first capitolo of the *Trionfo della morte*, while *Voi ch'ascoltate in rime sparse* (xv, 15) opens the canzoniere. The fruits of Monteverdi's riper years, they allow us to see him in a serious yet peaceful mood that is

far removed from the tension and tumult of the warlike madrigals.[6]

6. Pirrotta (*Scelte poetiche*, p. 62) considers the Petrarch settings as part of a deep and personal secret of the composer, and in view of their context in Book VI and in the *Selva morale* this can hardly be doubted.

# 6

# *Canzonette*

Of the twenty-five canzonette written during the composer's youth, all but four were published in the 1584 collection. Although they require only a vocal trio, they are not easy to perform because the ubiquitous *chiavette* demand downward transposition for modern comfort, and each singer needs specially copied parts (if the errors attendant on internal repeats are to be avoided) with a sensible underlay of the residual text. Musicians of earlier times were used to improvising such matters. The set begins with a dedicatory piece, *Qual si può dir* (x, 1), which puns on the name of Monteverdi's Cremonese patron, Pietro Ambrosini; and the final number is a typical envoi telling the songs to go their own sweet way. *Hor, care canzonette* (x, 24) launches itself with an unmistakable hemiola pattern—a sure sign that Monteverdi was already aching to escape from the four-square limitations of the classical canzonetta.

Ex. 12

Hor ca - re can - zo - net - te, Si - cu - ra - men te an - dre - te

He turned nevertheless to earlier compositions for his poetry, which seems to be largely drawn from anthologies published between 1566 and 1581.[1] Two of his own songs begin with the words *Chi vuol veder* (x, 14 and 20), but neither poem has any further connection with the Petrarch sonnet sharing the same incipit.[2] At 17, Monteverdi was not ready for the emotional demands of such a poet, nor was the canzonetta the right place for such an experiment. The light verses he chose, so full of references to mythical or historical characters of ancient Greece and Rome, were destined for a polite, even convivial end—the delectation of amateur musicians.

They enjoyed sufficient success, however, to inspire four more, which appeared in 1594 in a collection assembled by Antonio Morsolino, a composer whom he must surely have known in Cremona.[3] Thereafter unaccompanied canzonette vanish from view until he mentions them in a letter to Duke Ferdinando at Mantua (March 2, 1624) in connection with the growing musical appetite of Cesare I d'Este, Duke of Modena, who thanks the composer on March 24 and July 4 of the same year for sending certain pieces of music, and expresses an interest

1. Pirrotta, *Scelte poetiche*, p. 5.
2. Frati, "Il Petrarca," p. 65.
3. First transcribed and discussed in *C. Monteverdi, 12 Compositioni Vocali. . .*, ed. Wolfgang Osthoff (Milan, 1958). See also Osthoff, "Monteverdi-Funde," *Archiv für Musikwissenschaft* 14 (1957):253.

in his canzonette for three voices.[4] Although no titles are mentioned in these letters, a canzonetta corresponding to this description in the archives at Modena —*Ahi, che si partì il mio bel sol* (xvi, 542)—is in all probability the one sent from Venice in 1624.

---

4. Henry Prunières, *Monteverdi* (New York, 1926), p. 217. The last mention of a canzonetta in Monteverdi's correspondence occurs in a letter dated February 23, 1630.

# 7
# *Trios with Continuo*

Just as in his youth he had been invited to contribute to Cremonese anthologies, so in his middle years Monteverdi was asked for the occasional canzonetta by a Mantuan or Venetian on the verge of publishing. But his main output appeared in the *Scherzi musicali* of 1607, the posthumously published *Madrigali e canzonette*, and the heterogeneous Books VII and VIII. The Mantuan set contains a ballet of his as well as two scherzi by his younger brother, but the prevailing texture is absolutely constant: two soprano voices and a bass, doubled by two violins and basso continuo instruments as available. Most of the lyrics are by Gabriello Chiabrera, whose innovative and anacreontic verse forms rejoice in Monteverdi's zestful settings, alive with cross-rhythms and hemiolas that are almost totally obscured in modern versions. Just as the introductory Sinfonia and Aria in Act II of *Orfeo* was misbarred in countless editions, so the natural word-accents of a work such as *Vaghi rai di cigli ardenti* (x, 46) have been distorted by a regrettable penchant on the part of editors for a pedantic *Vierhebigkeit* that is far removed from the composer's intentions. Even the most cursory glance at the bass line of ritornel and verse is sufficient to reveal the true metrical scheme:

Ex. 13    Ritornel

Va-ghi  rai  di ci- gliar-den- ti,  più lu-  cen- ti  che del  Sol  non so- noi  ra- i

The *Scherzi* rank as vocal trio-sonatas, framed and elegantly accompanied by the two-violin-and-continuo combination that was to play such an important part in Monteverdi's later music, whether sacred, secular, or occasional. Like *Orfeo*, the premiere of which took place in the year of their publication,[1] the *Scherzi* were dedicated to Prince Francesco Gonzaga, and first charmed courtly audiences at the concerts given in his apartments.

In complete contrast, four trios from Book VII and three from Book VIII are polyphonically animated and entirely through-composed. Another belonging to this category is *Taci, Armelin* (ix, 106), found in a collection of pieces based on poems by G. B. Anselmi of Treviso. A small dog named Armelin (Ermine, probably because of a white coat dappled with black) persists in barking and bothering his master, who is intent upon amorous

1. They were successful enough to warrant republication in 1609, 1615, and 1628.

pursuits.[2] The mounting wrath of the frustrated lover is admirably suggested by two-part rhythmic counterpoint over a three-part texture:

*Ogni amante è guerrier* (viii, 88) draws upon a text originally written by Rinuccini in honor of Henry IV of

2. An apparently more docile dog, with which Monteverdi must have been familiar, is depicted in a painting by an unknown artist (probably Mantuan) and illustrated in Elia Santoro, *Iconografia Monteverdiana* (Cremona, 1968), plate 18. With the composer are two young men of noble dress and bearing, possibly Francesco and Vincenzo II Gonzaga, and another, younger man, who could perhaps be Guilio Cesare Monteverdi. The artistic relationship between the Gonzaga brothers and the Monteverdi brothers was at its closest from about 1605 until 1611. Santoro questions the authenticity of the portrait, partly because Monteverdi was a performer on the viola da braccio, but the instrument depicted in his hand is considerably larger than a viola. G. C. Monteverdi, however, in his *Dichiaratione* (1607) reminds us that his elder brother's duties included playing the viola bastarda. Larger than the tenor viol and smaller than the bass viol, the viola bastarda was an instrument with six or seven strings, well suited for playing chords and rapid passages. Although only five strings can be detected in the painting, it is almost certainly one of these instruments that Monteverdi is holding.

France,[3] and its four separate sections—differently scored, but reuniting in a trio at the end—declaim in heroic or narrative manner the attributes of Ferdinand III. *Gira il nemico insidioso* (viii, 75) compares Love to a dangerous enemy who must be fought back by armed force and cavalry charge. Monteverdi's familiarity with Italian trumpet calls such as the *buttasella* and *accavallo* is clearly proved when his musical motives are compared with the actual signals.[4]

Ex. 15

A droll sense of humor and a lively imagination combine to make this trio just as amusing as some of the earlier ones (and possibly more engaging) because of the way in which the interest builds up as the six sections progress. The three strophic trios at the end of the *madrigali amorosi* hark back almost to the mood of the *Scherzi* of 1607, and at least one of the texts was attractive enough to prompt another and quite different setting in Book IX —*Su su su, pastorelli vezzosi* (ix, 89)

Apart from the two spiritual trios in the *Selva morale* (one of them with ritornels for strings, again after the fashion of the *Scherzi*), nothing appeared in print until the posthumously published Book IX, which contains ten trios of considerable charm and newness of form.

3. Pirrotta, *Scelte poetiche di Monteverdi*, p. 56, n. 128.
4. See the "Italienische Signale" in *Das Erbe Deutscher Musik I* (*Reichsdenkmale*), vol. 7—*Trompetenfanfaren* (Kassel, 1936):68.

Although most of them are scored for men's voices, two are for alto, tenor, and bass, and one calls for two sopranos and alto. A favored pattern seems to be the one adopted for *Alcun non mi consigli* (ix, 42), which allows each of the three voices in turn to sing a solo. The melodies are different but the bass line remains constant. Each verse is followed by a refrain, always with identical music and text. The straightforward strophic song is represented by works such as *Quando dentro al tuo seno* (ix, 56) and even if this contains no solo passages there is still a vestige of a refrain, which in this particular piece always leads back to the beginning of the next verse:

Ex. 16

*Non voglio amare* (ix, 58) gives every intention of following this procedure, but takes a divergent course in its use of solo phrases pitted against duetting replies. The irresistible touch of a cool breeze pervades *Come dolce oggi l'auretta spira* (ix, 60), which originally formed part of Monteverdi's setting of Strozzi's *Proserpina rapita* in 1630. The harmony is often deliciously wanton in spite of its uncomplicated appearance, as also in the second half of *Perchè, se m'odiavi* (ix, 79), of which there is a related solo setting in 1634.[5] (See Ex. 17)

5. Facsimiles and transcriptions from Vincenti's anthology were first made available by Domenico de Paoli in *Claudio Monteverdi* (Milan, 1945), Appendix.

Ex. 17

ti  fè  co - sì  bel - la,  si  fer - ra,  si_al -

te - ra  per  l'al - ma_im - pia - gar - mi.

# 8

# *Duets*

Monteverdi's duets for voices and continuo emerged
naturally from the style of the *Scherzi* of 1607, and it is
clear that Venetian musical fashions subsequently helped
that emergence to a not inconsiderable extent. The bass
voice is omitted for the simple reason that its text is
carried by the upper voices and its melody by the
continuo. Thus freed from a distant partner, the paired
voices (usually two tenors or two sopranos) can behave
independently or combine at will, playing off imitative
introductions against melting chains of thirds or sixths.
Even so, the pattern is not so rigid as to preclude all
innovations. *Non è di gentil core* (vii, 8) reflects the
ballata form chosen by Guarini[1] in an extended reprise of

1. Not, as often stated, by "Francesca degli Atti." This error seems to go back to the
Monteverdi article in the fifth edition of Grove's Dictionary (London, 1954). There
was, however, a singer named Francesco degli Atti (a member of the Archduke Ferdinand's court chapel at Graz), who set this lyric in the early years of the seventeenth
century and had it published in Bartolomeo Cesana's *Musiche a una doi e tre voci*
(Venice, 1613). For further information on degli Atti, see Hellmut Federhofer, "Graz
Court Musicians and their contributions to the *Parnassus Musicus Ferdinandaeus*
(1615)," *Musica Disciplina* 9 (1955):167.

the opening musical paragraph. *Dice la mia bellissima Licori* (vii, 58) is unusual in its nonimitative beginning and its frequent change of meter illustrating the phrase *no 'l posso toccar,* but perhaps the most remarkable of all is the setting not of a madrigal text, but of a sonnet — Guarini's *Interrotte speranze* (vii, 94). Counterpoint being almost entirely absent, Monteverdi gives us in its place a homorhythmic type of declamation somewhat reminiscent of the *Pastor Fido* madrigals. What is more, he plays most skillfully with the possibilities of recurring unisons in the voice parts:

Always ready to take slight liberties with verse form for the sake of his music, Monteverdi brings in the words *Donna crudel* in such a way as to interfere with the scheme of the sonnet if his interpolation is taken literally or written down thoughtlessly. But a careful study of passages suggesting a conflict between poetry and music invariably shows that he devoted much more thought to such matters than is generally common among his modern exegetists.

The best-known duet in Book VII, *Chiome d'oro* (vii,

176), is really a canzonetta decked out with ritornels scored for a trio-sonata combination. While the instrumental and vocal melodies go their own delightful way, they are united by the lightsome tread of a bass line whose contours seem to weld together all the various elements. The power of an organizing bass line can also be felt in the setting of Bernardo Tasso's *Ohimè, dov'è il mio ben?* (vii, 152), in which the four short sections are united by a romanesca type of of ostinato kept at a suitably subliminal level by the harpsichord and cello.[2]

*O come vaghi* (ix, 102), a tenor duet similar to those in Book VII, appeared in the same volume as *Taci, Armelin*, and is also based on a poem by Anselmi. His publisher, Bartolomeo Magni, was responsible for the *Scherzi musicali* of 1632, a small volume containing two duets of great fame: the chaconne *Zefiro torna* (ix, 9)[3] on a sonnet of Rinuccini, and *Armato il cor* (ix, 27). Both were reprinted in Book IX, and *Armato il cor* also in Book VIII, which may be considered as proof of the regard in which they were universally held. *Zefiro* is a model of economy and resource, of discipline and freedom, of outward calm and inner passion. Although the harmonic shock at the third appearance of the word *piango* is too familiar to need quotation, it has hitherto not been noticed that the final cadenza provides an elegantly and fully written out example of a *ribattuto della gola* and of a *trillo*, in both voices:

Ex. 19

[a]

2. Translated, somewhat freely, for the Marenzio setting, which Thomas Watson included in his *First Sett of Italian Madrigalls Englished* (London, 1590).

3. Not to be confused with the Petrarch text set to music in Book VI. The first line of Rinuccini's sonnet is slightly modified by Monteverdi, who substitutes *accenti* for *odori*.

Four tenor duets, again in the style of Book VII, were published in the *Madrigali guerrieri, et amorosi* of 1638, but Monteverdi's careful allocation of two duets to each genre is obscured by the appearance of all four as a group in the modern collected edition.[4] *Armato il cor* opens with a clear demonstration of the flowing nature of metrical relationships, the subtlety of which may be appreciated visually by a deliberately exaggerated reduction of note-values:[5]

Ex. 20

Ar - ma - toil cor, ar - ma - toil cor, ar - ma - toil

cor d'a - da - man - ti - na fe - de nel - l'a - mo - ro - so

Any account of Monteverdi's treatment of the sonnet form would have to take into consideration the oddly disposed *O sia tranquillo il mar* (ix, 36), which devotes virtually the first half of the piece to the first eleven lines, and the second half to the last tercet. It goes without saying that the two halves differ considerably in their approach to the poem — recitative at first, then a lilting arioso, with a final return to descriptive declamation. It may be a strange way to deal with a classical verse form, but the result is sheer charm, not unmixed with surprises.

Such qualities, overlaid with a patina of sheer virtuosity, occur in *Mentre vaga Angioletta* (viii, 246), which is a musical setting of a poem about music, and in particular about a lady singer whose name may be hinted

4. Malipiero placed them in Vol. IX in order to reduce the bulk of Vol. VIII. See his bibliographical note: ix, 101.
5. The two tenor lines are reversed in ix, 27.

at in the opening phrase.[6] Unusually for a continuo composition, the introductory solo is unaccompanied, the harpsichord entering only when "Musico spirto prende" is sung. Thereafter the two tenors illustrate in amazingly vivid manner every word or expression used by Guarini to describe the singer's art, besides supplying incidentally a magnificent summary of vocal ornamentation as it was known and practiced in Monteverdi's time.

6. Guarini's title was *Gorga di cantatrice*. He lived long enough to hear Adriana Basile in her prime, and it is interesting to note that she is called "Angioletta" in poems by the Duke of Laurenzana and Fulvio Testi, as well as in a letter of Abbot Grillo.

# 9

# *Songs with Continuo*

The frequently distorted view of a composer's work that can be given by too great a reliance on publication dates is nowhere more clearly shown than in the case of Monteverdi's monody. No examples of accompanied song survive from the period prior to 1619, when Book VII was brought out, yet it must be clear from his artistic association with virtuoso singers at Mantua, such as Rasi, Campagnolo, Adriana Basile, and her sister Margherita, that he wrote solos for them and heard them perform as described in his letters.[1]

By 1609 Monteverdi tended to think first in terms of song, and only second in terms of a polyphonic setting, whenever he was commissioned to set words to music. In the letter to Striggio dated August 24, 1609, he announces his intention of setting a poem "ad una voce sola," but

1. Rasi is mentioned in Monteverdi's letter dated December 9, 1916. The name of Campagnolo appears in correspondence from the years 1608, 1620, 1624, 1627; and that of Adriana Basile in 1610, 1611, 1616, 1617, 1620, 1623.

if the duke does not approve, he will rearrange it for five voices. Angelo Grillo, sending him a letter of thanks in 1610 for setting one of his pious poems as a solo song, mentions two particular artists who would do justice to it: Francesco Campagnolo and Adriana Basile.[2] These virtuosi may even have inspired the two most luxurious monodies in Book VII — *Temprò la cetra* (vii, 1) and *Con che soavità* (vii, 137). The first, scored for tenor and continuo, with five-part symphonies and ritornels by way of framework, glorifies the sonnet that opens the third part of Marini's *La Lira* (Venice, 1614). The conflict of war and love rears its double head long before the *Madrigali guerrieri, et amorosi*, but by the end of the first quatrain we known that Love will be the victor. The last few measures of the opening symphony provide the material for the ritornels, and the final lines of the sonnet lead to two further repeats of the symphony, separated by a dancelike episode.[3] To this impression of balanced unity the vocal sections add their own contribution, for their bass line is constant in contour if not in actual length. The kind of ornamentation considered appropriate for a dedicatory work is readily apparent, for the purpose of *Temprò la cetra* was to open Book VII with a flourish:

Ex. 21

tem - pran- do i fe    -                -

ri    se -    gni

2. Alfred Einstein, "Abbot Angelo Grillo's Letters as Source Material for Music History," *Essays on Music* (New York, 1956), p. 175. This is a translation of an article originally written for the *Kirchenmusikalisches Jahrbuch* in 1911.
3. For evidence in favor of the fact that this work was intended as a ballet, see Reinhart Strom, "Osservazioni su 'Tempro la cetra,' " *Rivista Italiana di Musicologia* 2 (1967): 357-64.

*Con che soavità,* although a unique and memorable example of the way in which poet and musician can meet together harmoniously, was almost certainly composed after Guarini's death. A soprano voice, a central jewel, is set in the midst of a tripartite harmonic structure consisting of a small group of plucked instruments (two archlutes, a harpsichord, and a spinet); a string quartet with its own harpsichord; and a consort of three viols, the top two being designated "da braccio overo da gamba." Monteverdi's choice was surely the softer-toned viola da gamba, whose deep register, supported perhaps by a small pipe organ, would offer wonderful contrasts to the plucked or bold sonorities of the other groups. These variously beautiful colors alternate and combine in a kaleidophonic surge of sound, affecting the voice but never obscuring it, illuminating the text without ever being intrusive. "La bella Adriana" must have known and sung this work, even if she did not actually breathe it into being.

Typical Venetian monodies begin to appear in Milanuzzi's collection (1624), though there is no lack of inventiveness and imagination. *Ohimè ch'io cado* (ix, 111) takes a six-verse poem and sets it in the form of a variation chain over a bass that depends on an unusual pattern of five-bar phrases—three in succession, rounded off by one of six bars. An internal melodic repeat produces a form (ABB'C) suggesting a neater degree of symmetry than one might expect from a period of 21 units. *La mia turca* (ix, 117) and *Sì dolce è il tormento* (ix, 119) also explore a tempting vein of amorous badinage, their very simplicity rendering the melodies indelible. This is also true of the shorter songs in the *Scherzi musicali* of 1632, a choice anthology containing two variants of a favorite chaconne pattern. One is found in the duet *Zefiro torna* (ix, 9), the other in *Quel sguardo sdegnosetto* (x, 77), which hints more closely at the relationship in the instrumental linking passage before the third section:

Ex. 22

Zefiro

Quel sguardo

Another work based on the chaconne, and possibly written in the early 1630s, is *Voglio di vita uscir*,[4] a lover's lament couched in a *sdrucciolo* verse form that results from a recurring use of third-person-plural verbs. *Ed è pur dunque vero* (x, 82) is unusual in that it joins an instrumental line (presumably violin) to the recitativelike vocal part. But the form is akin to that of *Ohimè, ch'io cado*, being built on ground-bass patterns that provide strength to the harmonic argument and an impression of unity to the composition as a whole. *Ecco di dolci raggi* (x, 81) was separated, in the original publication, from its second verse (x, 91), but Camarella's reprint of 1633 brought the two together. Monteverdi's only surviving song with ritornels for two violins and continuo seems to be the strophic aria *Più lieto il guardo*.[5]

The moving and expressive *Lamento d'Olimpia*[6] may belong either to the composer's second decade in Venice, when he was at the height of his powers, or to a somewhat earlier date in Mantua, where he is known to have written

4. Osthoff, *12 Compositioni Vocali*, p. 18. The same chaconne theme is used in one of Monteverdi's psalms for solo voice and continuo, at the words *laudate eum* in *Laudate Dominum* (xv, 753).
5. de Paoli, *Monteverdi*, Appendix.
6. Osthoff, *12 Compositioni Vocali*, p. 10.

several laments. In either case, the work could have been intended for the golden voice of Adriana Basile, who remained in the service of the Gonzaga for some years after Monteverdi left, continuing to sing works tht he wrote for her, as his letters indicate. Olimpia, a princess from the Low Countries, plays a minor but significant role in canti IX, X, and XI of Ariosto's *Orlando Furioso*, but the text for this lament is by an unknown poet. Whether or not it ever formed part of a stage work is impossible to determine.

# II
# RELIGIOUS MUSIC

# *10*
# *Introduction*

Not all of Monteverdi's religious music can be called church music, for on his own admission certain works were intended for performance in the private apartments of distinguished men, while on the evidence of the texts certain other works rank as paraliturgical motets rather than formal settings from the breviary or missal. Like his madrigals, these religious compositions embrace his entire artistic career, yet their dates of publication are often much later than their period of origin. The following discussions are therefore arranged according to genre, the list of first editions being given for reference only. Entries in italics denote anthologies.

| Date | Short Title (compiler) | Dedicatee/*Contents* |
|------|------------------------|----------------------|
| 1582 | Sacrae Cantiunculae | Dom Stefano Caninio (Valcarengo)[1] |
| 1610 | Sanctissimae Virgini Missa. . . | Pope Paul V (Rome) |
| *1615* | *Parnassus musicus Ferdin-andaeus* (Bonometti) | *one motet* |
| *1620* | *Libro primo de motetti* (Bianchi) | *four motets* |
| *1620* | *Libro secondo de motetti* (Bianchi) | *Litany* |
| *1621* | *Symbolae diversorum musicorum* (Calvo)[2] | *two motets* |
| *1622* | *Promptuarii musici concentus* [I] (Donfrid) | *one motet* |
| *1624* | *Seconda raccolta de' sacri canti* (Calvo) | *three motets* |
| *1625* | *Sacri Affetti* (Sammaruco) | *one motet* |
| *1625* | *Ghirlanda sacra* (Simonetti) | *four motets* |
| *1627* | *Promptuarii musici concentus* [III] (Donfrid) | *one motet* |
| *1627* | *Psalmi de Vespere* (Sabino) | *one psalm* |
| *1629* | *Quarta raccolta de' canti sacri* (Calvo) | *two motets* |
| 1641 | Selva morale e spirituale | Eleonora Gonzaga (Vienna) |
| *1645* | *Motetti a voce sola* | *one motet* |
| 1650 | Messa. . .Salmi. . .Letanie | Dom Odoardo Baranardi (Venice)[3] |
| *1651* | *Raccolta di motetti* (Casati) | *two motets* |

The above list does not include sacred contrafacta of madrigals by Coppini, Lappi, and Profe. It does, however, show that Monteverdi's religious music, properly considered, gained a ready entry into the best collections published in Venice from the time he arrived there to take up the post of director of music at St. Mark's, until a few years after his death in 1643.

1. Near Acquanegra, in the district of Cremona.
2. The basso continuo part is dated 1620, the others 1621.
3. Abbot of the congregation of Camaldolese monks, and priest of S. Maria delle Carceri, Venice.

# 11
# *Masses*

Don Bassano Casola, assistant director of music to
Vincenzo Gonzaga, wrote in 1610[1] of the forthcoming
collection of sacred music by Monteverdi that it began
with a six-part mass, of great complexity, based on eight
(actually ten) themes from Nicholas Gombert's motet *In
illo tempore*. When it was completed, the parts were sent
to Venice for publication, and a presentation copy for
Pope Paul V was taken by the composer to Rome, where
he hoped to obtain a grant for his elder son's education.
Although his plea fell on deaf ears, his music did not; and
the rebindings of the choirbook show that the mass was
performed and kept in use for many years. In the mean-
time, German publishers borrowed movements from the
Venetian edition, with the result that Monteverdi —
previously known mainly as a madrigalist — found himself
successfully launched as a composer of church music.

1. To Cardinal Ferdinando Gonzaga. See Vogel, "Claudio Monteverdi," *Vierteljahrsschrift für Musikwissenschaft* 3 (1887): 430.

The *Missa in illo tempore* (xiv, 57) belongs to that category of masterpieces which is theoretically well known but actually misunderstood.[2] It has, for instance, never been explained why a parody mass should appear in a collection of pieces for feasts of the Blessed Virgin, or why that particular motet by Gombert was chosen. The explanation is that when Monteverdi first came to Mantua he worked closely with Giaches de Wert, a master of northern polyphony and a skilled hand where the parody mass was concerned, as his *Missa Transeunte Domino* clearly demonstrates. In addition, many of de Wert's motets make use of entire Gospel texts from the missal, as was formerly the custom.[3]

The three words "in illo tempore" point unequivocally to the fact that we are dealing with a liturgical Gospel text, and the continuation "loquente Jesu ad turbas" indicates the feasts for which both motet and mass were intended: the Vigil of the Assumption, the Nativity of the Blessed Virgin Mary, and at Saturday masses that formed part of her commemorative office.[4] Apart from a temporary reduction to four voices for the "Crucifixus," the texture of Monteverdi's mass is sonorous and luxuriant, expanding to seven voices for the final "Agnus Dei." The continuo part, although something of a novelty

2. See H. F. Redlich, introductory notes to the Eulenburg edition (Zurich, 1962). There is no reason to doubt the publication date of September 1, and even less reason to believe that Monteverdi "went hurriedly to Venice from where he wrote a letter on January 6, 1611." This date is a misreading, and should be 1617. Note that on p. vii, in the list of voice parts, "Sextapars" should replace "Tentaparo"; and in the text of the Gombert motet, "quaedam" must be substituted for "quendam," and "beati qui" for "beati quae."

3. See *Intravit Jesus*, for example, in the first book of five-part motets (Giaches de Wert, *Collected Works* [Rome, 1969], 11:84), which sets the complete Gospel for the Asusmption of the B.V.M. The critical notes in this volume are amplified and emended in *Notes* 32 (1975):126.

4. Although de Wert omitted the words *in illo tempore* at the beginning of his Gospel motets, many other composers retained them—Jean Mouton (*In illo tempore accesserunt*); Tielman Susato (*I.i.t. cum audissent*); J. van Berchem (*I.i.t. dixit Jesus*), to give only three instances.

at the time of publication, would have been useful in holding things together.

Since there are numerous references to masses in the composer's correspondence, it is all the more disappointing that so few have survived. In 1616 he mentions a mass for Christmas Eve, in 1618 a concerted mass for the Feast of the Most Precious Blood and another for Ascension Day. For the obsequies of Cosimo II, Grand Duke of Tuscany, at the church of SS Giovanni e Paolo on May 25, 1621, he composed an introductory motet *(O vos omnes,* paraphrasing the Holy Saturday antiphon and a passage from Lamentations 5:3), the Introit *Requiem aeternam* — both sung by his son Francesco — as well as the *Dies Irae, De profundis,* and some responsories.[5] Letters of 1621 and 1627 mention a "messa solenne" and a mass for Christmas Eve, it being the custom for the director of music to write a new one every year at this season. Unfortunately, no trace of any such work survives from the period 1616 to 1627, and the two masses published later cannot be confidently assigned to any particular year. There is, however, an isolated *Gloria*[6] in manuscript, whose double choir layout (with separate parts for two organs) suggests that Monteverdi may have written it especially for St. Mark's.

It was in the basilica that a mass of thanksgiving was offered on November 28, 1631, when the city had recovered from a serious outbreak of the plague,[7] and a

5. Vogel, "Claudio Monteverdi," p. 377.
6. Osthoff, *12 Compositioni Vocali,* p. 65. The editor suggests that this work might be dated not earlier than 1620, and points to the thematic links between the opening and closing settings of the word *gloria,* which are also a feature of the *Gloria concertata a 7* assigned to the year 1631. In fact the date may well be nearer 1630 than 1620.
7. Monteverdi's former literary collaborator and constant friend, Alessandro Striggio, died of the plague when he visited Venice to enlist help for the beseiged city of Mantua. Monteverdi's son Francesco is sometimes named as a victim, but he must have survived, because he sang two roles in the opera *Ermiona* (Felice Sances) when it was given at Padua in 1636. See B. Brunelli, *I Teatri di Padova* (Padua, 1921), p. 73.

report by one who was present confirms that the *Gloria* and *Credo,* by Monteverdi, sounded fourth with "trombe squarciate"—probably slide-trumpets or narrow-bore trombones.[8] These two movements were eventually, though imperfectly, published in the *Selva morale* of 1641. The *Gloria* (xv, 117), which is the only surviving complete example of Monteverdi's concertato mass style, calls for seven-part choir, six soloists, string orchestra, and trombones. As regards the *Credo,* however, the tutti sections were mislaid at some time between 1631 and 1640, so that all the printer received was a handful of vocal and instrumental parts for three solo sections: "Crucifixus," "Et resurrexit," and "Et iterum" (xv, 178). To save face it was given out that these fragments could be used to replace the corresponding sections in the *Messa a 4 voci da cappella* (xv, 59), which has misled generations of Monteverdi scholars and performers.[9] Not only are the fragments in a style totally different from that of the four-part mass; they do not fit as regards tonality, time signatures, or vocal scoring. But they do agree with the luxuriant texture of the *Gloria.*

8. Vogel, "Claudio Monteverdi," p. 393. See also the discussion of "trombe squarciate" in *Claudio Monteverdi e il suo tempo* (Verona, 1969), p. 433. A reliable performing edition of the *Gloria,* by John Steele, is published in the Penn State Music Series, No. 18 (University Park, 1968).

9. Eulenburg miniature score No. 990 (London, 1962), in which Denis Arnold writes of the "strange interpolations" in the original form of the mass. But the wording in the part-books merely states that at certain points you may sing the alternate versions if you wish. These are not interpolated; they appear elsewhere in the volumes. The "original" movements are therefore not omitted from Arnold's edition; they are (quite correctly) included.

The *Messa a 4 voci* is a sober and uneventful work, possibly intended for use at one of the smaller churches in Venice, for its manner harks back to the late sixteenth century, despite the continuo part. A single short motive, of secular rather than sacred cast, appears throughout the mass; and the possibility that Monteverdi borrowed this time from one of his own madrigals should not be entirely ruled out.

A second *Messa a 4 voci da cappella* (xvi, 1) appeared in the posthumously published volume of 1650. Its character, differing markedly from that of its predecessor, contrasts passages of elaborately beautiful counterpoint of a baroque persuasion with exuberant chordal sections in a lilting tripla context.[10]

10. For a perceptive musical analysis of this work, see Reginald Smith Brindle, "Monteverdi's G Minor Mass: An Experiment in Construction," *The Musical Quarterly* 54 (1968):352.

# 12
# *Vespers of the Blessed Virgin Mary*

From June until October, 1595, Monteverdi and a few of
his colleagues in the ducal chapel were ordered to join the
Mantuan army's expedition to Hungary, the main object
of which was to thrust back the Turkish army then
occupying key positions on the road to Budapest. It was
the composer's first taste of campaign conditions, weari-
some travel, and foreign habits. But he made the most of
it, and his warlike madrigals of 1638 benefited from
emotion recollected in tranquillity. He may also have had
some practice in composing church music, for the official
campaign chronicler mentions that the musicians sang
vespers with organ accompaniment after the court had
done justice to a handsome supper.[1] But since his earliest

1. Vincenzo Errante, "Forse che sì, forse che no," *Archivio Storico Lombardo, Serie
Quinta* 42 (1915), p. 31.

extant letter says that he, as director of Vincenzo's chapel (not Santa Barbara), would welcome greater opportunity for providing masses and motets, it may be assumed that prior to 1601 his main concern was with secular music.

In spite of the tumultuous events of the next eight years, Monteverdi was able to compose five psalms, a hymn, two Magnificats, and a few motets, and these he published together with a mass in 1610. The psalms are those proper to the usual office of the Blessed Virgin, and to her major feastdays: *Dixit Dominus, Laudate pueri, Laetatus sum, Nisi Dominus, Lauda Jerusalem,* and the same is true of the hymn, *Ave maris stella.* Given two settings of the *Magnificat,* a choirmaster could prepare a different setting for first and second vespers, or select the one most appropriate for his vocal and instrumental resources.

The sequence of items begins with *Domine ad adjuvandum* (xiv, 123),[2] a fully orchestrated response to the intonation "Deus in adjutorium meum intende," and it is both a reminder and a reworking of the introductory toccata to *Orfeo.* Since the intonation is mostly on one note, and the toccata on a double pedal, they fit together very well. In complete contrast, the psalms make use of genuine choral polyphony, brilliant passages for solo voices and groups of soloists, instrumental interludes, and integrated structural devices. *Dixit Dominus* (xiv, 133) takes, for its main melodic basis, the plainchant for Tone 4 (with the ending A) transposed down a fourth, which

2. See also the Novello edition (London, 1961) for the response, psalms, hymn, and seven-part Magnificat. The six-part Magnificat is available in an edition by K. Matthaei (Bärenreiter). Further on the Vespers, see S. Bonta, "Liturgical Problems . . . ," *Journal of the A.M.S.* 20 (1967):87; W. Osthoff, "Unità liturgica e artistica," *Rivista Italiana di Musicologia* 2 (1967): 314.

makes its first appearance at the initial entry of the second soprano:

Ex. 26

Di - xit_ Do- mi-nus Do - mi- no me - o: se - de a dex - tris me - is.

The second half of the verse enlarges upon a formula found in Viadana's *Cento concerti ecclesiastici*, where numerous examples are given of embroidered psalm verses in falsobordone.[3] But where Viadana writes a flourish in the style of a Conforto or a Bovicelli, Monteverdi allows billowing counterpoint to carry the melisma to its appointed cadence:

Ex. 27a (Viadana)

Donec ponam inimicos tu -

os.

3. Lodovico Grossi da Viadana, *Cento concerti ecclesiastici*, ed. C. Gallico (Verona, 1964), p. 92.

Ex. 27b (Monteverdi)

The psalm follows this pattern verse by verse until the doxology, where a straightforward contrast of solo and polyphony brings the movement to a close. *Laudate pueri* (xiv, 153) calls for two choirs of equal tessiturae, the sole support being the organ, whereas in the previous psalm an instrumental group provided short interludes and (presumably) some doubling of the vocal lines. Monteverdi gives shape to *Laetatus sum* (xiv, 174) by alternating, in the bass part, a "walking motive" (based on the *Ruggiero* theme), a slower and more conjunct theme, and a pedal section. The recurrence of these elements at set intervals lends the psalm great cohesion and strength.

*Nisi Dominus* (xiv, 198) appears to be cast in the form of a double-choir setting with five parts on each side, but

since the first tenor of Choir I sings the same music as the
second tenor of Choir II, the massive polyphonic passages
are for nine voices only. The doubling of tenor parts is
due to the fact that these carry the psalm-tone (6F) and the
composer obviously wanted it to be heard. There is much
dialogue between the two sides, as in the final psalm
*Lauda Jerusalem* (xiv, 237), which follows a similar plan
with regard to the tone-bearing tenor lines. And there are
junctures at which the pattern of rapidly superimposed
sequences brings about spicy harmonic clashes:

*Ave maris stella* (xiv, 274), sheltering the hymn melody with great tenderness, offers a variety of vocal scoring and instrumental interludes that could be played by strings and wind in alternation.[4] In the seven-part *Magnificat* (xiv, 285) Monteverdi allows himself the luxury of an orchestra consisting of strings, cornetti, recorders, flutes, and trombones, whose function is more often to provide ritornels than to support the solo voices, though there are some highly effective obbligato passages in "Quia respexit" and "Deposuit." The trails of glory in the doxology, floating back from an echo tenor, belong to the loftiest flights of a remarkable musical mind. The six-part *Magnificat* (xiv, 327) requires no instruments other than the organ, but the variations of vocal color and ornament seem to be almost inexhaustible.

Since the *Selva morale* contains only two of the five psalms needed for a complete polyphonic office of the B.V.M., it cannot properly be considered a Marian collection in the same way as the anthology of 1610. In churches where it was customary to sing only the first psalm (*Dixit Dominus*) and the *Magnificat* in polyphony, it would of course be perfectly admissible to use the music in the *Selva*.[5] But for the closest comparison with 1610, we must turn to the posthumously published *Messa . . . Salmi . . . Letanie* of 1650. The five Marian psalms are well represented here, with a choice of two all the way down the list, except for *Laudate pueri*. Both settings of *Dixit Dominus* are for double choir, the second (xvi, 94) being by far the finer composition. This could go with the

4. Francisco Guerrero, in a document drawn up in 1586 for the chapter of Seville Cathedral, states that "always hearing the same instrument annoys the listener." See Robert Stevenson, *Spanish Cathedral Music in the Golden Age* (Berkeley and Los Angeles, 1961), p. 167.
5. On the custom of singing only one psalm in polyphony, see Frank d'Accone, "The Musical Chapels at the Florentine Cathedral and Baptistry. . . ," *Journal of the A.M.S.* 24 (1971):7.

single *Laudate pueri* (xvi, 211), and the second settings of *Laetatus sum* (xvi, 276), *Nisi Dominus* (xvi, 318), and *Lauda Jerusalem* (xvi, 358), to make a sequence of five psalms that largely agree with each other in matters of style and scoring.

With these features in common, they nevertheless show appreciable differences in other respects. *Dixit Dominus,* after the fashion of Willaert's psalms for two choirs, allows us to hear when a new verse begins by changing from one choir to the other, the two combining for phrases of special weight or significance. *Laudate pueri,* however, has no alternative but to reach a full close at the end of each verse, recommencing with a new idea, either harmonic or contrapuntal, for the following verse. At the "Sicut erat," Monteverdi allows himself a pun by going back to the opening theme, "as it was in the beginning:"

Ex. 29

Lau - da - te pu - e - ri Do - mi - num, lau - da - te no - men Do - mi - ni

Si - cut e - rat in prin - ci - pi - o, et nunc et sem - [per]

The same kind of punning recapitulation occurs in *Lauda Jerusalem,* where the psalm tone (3g) is given suitable prominence in the soprano part. Compared with this, the polyphony of *Laetatus sum* seems of a sober and majestic cast, in spite of the cheerful text of the psalm. *Nisi Dominus,* on the other hand, is rich in secular touches—an opening theme worthy of a popular song, unmistakable trumpet calls for "Surgite," and an almost operatic insistence on the word *non* of the righteous man who need entertain no fear of being confounded:

Ex. 30

non con-fun-de-tur, non, non, non. Be - a - tus vir

The other setting of *Laetatus sum* (xvi, 231)[6] demands resources of a far more opulent nature: six voices arranged in pairs (SS TT BB), with two violins, two trombones, and a bassoon. The first four notes of the *Laetatus sum* of 1610 are here used as an ostinato of unquenchable energy, but the G-g-c-d formula inevitably causes hundreds of perfect cadences, which Monteverdi makes little attempt to avoid. He accepts both the epigrammatic nature of the phrase-structure and the parallelism of the psalm verses, facing up to the V-I chords in a mood utterly different from his harmonically evasive approach to the *Lament of the Nymph*. In spite of the large score, his texture is by no means dense, the massive moments being saved for the doxology. In the chamber music setting of *Nisi Dominus* (xvi, 299), for STB, two violins and organ, the voices enjoy considerable independence as regards the manner (if not the theme) of their utterances, though they do combine now and again with the instruments for the sake of emphasis. *Lauda Jerusalem* (xvi, 344) is a virtuoso piece for male-voice trio and organ, rich in illustrative figures and in changes of meter.

6. Edited for practical use by James McKelvy (Mark Foster Music Co., 1967) Marquette, Mich.

# 13
# Vespers
# (de Tempore et de Sanctis)

In spite of Monsignor Biella's valiant attempt to penetrate the maze of Monteverdi's psalms,[1] the "Vespers" are still thought of in terms of one particular sequence of items, large or small as the case may be. Quite apart from the Vespers of the B.V.M. discussed above, the various psalms in the collections of 1641 and 1650 could be combined to make up sets for first vespers (and occasionally second vespers) as might be required:[2]

| DE TEMPORE | DE SANCTIS |
|---|---|
| The Nativity of Our Lord (1) | St. Mark (1) |

1. "I Vespri dei Santi di Claudio Monteverdi," *Musica Sacra* 90 (1966):144.
2. This list is restricted to Doubles of the First Class, and to certain feasts of the second class that were given a higher rank at St. Mark's. *Credidi* was required only for All Saint's Day (2d vespers), the Holy Name of Jesus (both vespers), and for Martyrs. *Memento Domine David* would have been needed for vespers of confessors and bishops.

| | |
|---|---|
| The Holy Name of Jesus (1&2) | Finding of the Holy Cross (1&2) |
| Epiphany (1) | Nativity of John Baptist (1&2) |
| Ascension (1&2) | SS Peter and Paul (1) |
| Whitsunday (1) | Most Precious Blood (1&2) |
| Trinity Sunday (1) | St. Michael (1) |
| | All Saints (1&2) |

They could also be used for feasts of One Martyr, Several Martyrs, Confessors, Doctors, and Abbots. The only major feasts excluded from the present list are Easter, for which a setting of *In exitu Israel* would be needed, and Corpus Christi, which requires *Beati omnes*. Nevertheless, a remarkably large number of feast days could have been adorned with vocal and instrumental music of amazing variety and quality by drawing upon the psalms, the hymns, and the two Magnificats published in the *Selva morale* of 1641.[3]

Heterogeneous as this anthology may at first appear, a study of its orchestration reveals the fact that Monteverdi had two distinct sets of vespers in mind. One calls for a large choir, as many as eight soloists, a string orchestra, and three or four trombones.[4] The other rarely features soloists, and the maximum instrumental participation is a pair of violins here and there. Choirmasters, able to choose according to their musical resources, were always assured of artistic balance and cohesion as a final result. It should be noted, in addition, that it was customary to set only the first and last of the five psalms for double choir, so that *Dixit Dominus* usually calls for eight voices, and the same is true of *Laudate Dominum* (which stands last in order at most feasts), *Credidi* (required for 2d

3. Further details on liturgical music in Mantua: K. Jeppesen, "Monteverdi, Kappellmeister am S.ta Barbara?," *C.M. e il suo tempo* (Verona, 1969), p. 313; Pierre Tagmann, *Archivalische Studien zur Musikpflege am Dom von Mantua* (1500-1627), (Bern and Stuttgart, 1967).
4. The specified alternative instruments to trombones were viols, i.e., viole da braccia.

vespers of All Saints, both vespers for the Name of Jesus, and for 2d vespers of One Martyr and of Several Martyrs), and *Memento* (needed for the various feasts of Confessors and Doctors).

A closer glance at this proposed scheme shows that the orchestration tends to appear in a regular pattern of alternation if the items are placed in their proper liturgical order:

| | |
|---|---|
| *Dixit I* | double choir, soloists, strings, trombones[5] |
| *Confitebor II* | choir, soloists, violins[6] |
| *Beatus vir I* | choir, soloists, strings, trombones |
| *Laudate pueri I* | choir, soloists, violins |
| *Laudate Dom. II* | double choir, soloists, strings, [trombones][7] |

| | |
|---|---|
| Hymn | soloists, violins |
| *Magnificat I* | double choir, soloists, strings, trombones |

Similarly, a coherent pattern emerges from a list of the works demanding resources of a more modest type:

| | |
|---|---|
| *Dixit II* | double choir, soloists, violins |
| *Confitebor I* | five-part choir |
| *Beatus vir II* | five-part choir |
| *Laudate pueri II* | five-part choir |
| *Laudate Dom. III* | double choir, soloists[8] |

| | |
|---|---|
| Hymn | soloists, violins |
| *Magnificat II* | choir and chant, in alternation |

5. And, of course, basso continuo; this applies throughout the list.
6. Or, if preferable, *Confitebor III*, without violins.
7. Although no trombones are specified, they could be added in accordance with the accepted principles of doubling.
8. Or *Laudate I* a 6, with violins and trombones (or strings).

In his dedication of the *Selva* to Eleonora Gonzaga, the composer admits that the collection was not in so perfect a condition as he might have wished.[9] This is a fair remark in view of the fact that most of the *Credo a 7* is missing, two voice parts from *Magnificat I* seem likewise to have been mislaid, and a careful study of almost any item reveals some kind of confusion in the voice parts, so that many double-choir compositions and concertante effects are hidden, if not totally obscured. Be that as it may, Monteverdi has provided a more than ample grove of spiritual delights, most of which can be reconstructed in accordance with the known musico-liturgical practices of the time.

Among the scattered references to vesper psalms or services in Monteverdi's correspondence, one of the earliest is his offer of a *Dixit a 8*[10] to Vincenzo, Duke of Mantua, on March 26, 1611. He mentions the necessity of rehearsing solemn vespers for the Ascension ("Sensa" to the Venetians, and one of their most important feasts) in a letter dated April 21, 1618, to Don Vincenzo Gonzaga,[11] and relates to the Procurators at some length the scandal in the piazza just after vespers in honor of St. John of Alexandria, June 9, 1637.[12] In the longest of all his letters, written on March 13, 1620, and sent to Striggio at Mantua, he mentions payment of up to 50 ducats for looking after the music at one of the confrat-

9. See Denis Stevens, "Claudio Monteverdi: *Selva morale e spirituale*," *C.M. e il suo tempo*, p. 423.
10. This has frequently been mistranscribed as "Dixiat a 5," thus making the identification of the music difficult if not impossible.
11. Not to Alessandro Striggio, for whom the normal form of address was "Illustrissimo mio Signore. . . ." The inclusion of the word *Eccellentissimo* shows that the recipient was Don Vincenzo, the youngest son of Monteverdi's first patron.
12. More detailed information about this event is given by Francesco Sansovino, *Venetia Città Nobilissima* (Venice, 1663), pp. 22, 23.

ernities, the duties involving provision (or composition) of a mass and two vespers.[13]

Because of this constant demand for music, Monteverdi was now and again constrained to arrange what he had already written for a different group of vocalists or instrumentalists. That is why we have a reworking of the *Confitebor* of 1650; whereas the first version is for one soloist (xvi, 129), the revised setting is for two (xvi, 144).[14] An even more fascinating concordance has so far remained unnoticed because the two settings appear in different volumes. The first *Dixit Dominus* of 1641 (xv, 195) seems, at a casual glance, to be quite different from the first setting[15] of this psalm in 1650 (xvi, 54), for although they are both for eight voices, one has violins while the other relies simply on the organ. In addition, the psalms begin in completely different fashion. But the tutti sections for "Virgam virtutis" correspond, apart from very minor changes, and this is true for "Tecum principium" except that the bass entries in 1650 are relegated to the continuo part. "Dominus a dextris" also corresponds exactly, with the ruins toppling down in a thunderous homophonic tripla:

---

13. The verb *fare* can mean to create and to perform, and it is quite possible that Monteverdi composed the music that he subsequently directed. The director of music at St. Mark's was, in theory, not supposed to accept outside engagements, but it was doubtless possible to obtain special dispensation from time to time.
14. Jerome Roche, "Monteverdi—An Interesting Example of Second Thoughts," *The Music Review* 32 (1971): 193.
15. The double-choir disposition is correctly shown in xvi but not in xv, where the editor claims not to have found characteristic features of the *coro spezzato* style. They emerge quite clearly from a casual glance at pp. 206-7.

Several further correspondences indicate that the 1641 version is by far the more satisfactory of the two because of its richer texture, its more effective deployment of solo voices, and its stronger motivic feeling. With regard to the last-mentioned quality, one need only compare the evocative phrase for "exaltabit caput" in 1641 with its flabby counterpart of 1650:

Ex. 32 (a)

A different kind of reworking may be witnessed in the *Confitebor III* of 1641 (xv, 352). This time the overtones are suspiciously secular, and the instruction to perform the work either for five-part choir or for solo soprano and strings recalls the principle behind the *alla francese* madrigals, *Dolcissimo uscignuolo* and *Chi vuol haver felice*.[16] In fact Monteverdi draws on both madrigals to create an entirely different kind of composition—a contrafactum of considerable ingenuity, as the following examples show:

Ex. 33 (a)

Even more successful is the skillful injection of the quite unforgettable (and therefore immediately recognizable) ritornel from *Chiome d'oro* into the exposition of *Beatus vir* (xv, 368)[17] for six voices, two violins, and continuo. The music is expertly structured, with a contemplative middle section in triple time, solo voices taking over from the main chorus. Perhaps its most

16. See chap. 5. Redlich was of the opinion that this setting of *Confitebor* was included by Praetorius in his *Hymnodia Sionia* of 1611, but (as its title suggests) this volume contains only hymns. No *Confitebor* is to be found among the Latin words indexed in the final volume of Praetorius's collected works. See Redlich, *Claudio Monteverdi* (London, 1952,) pp. 138, 178.

17. Practical edition by John Steele (Novello, 1965).

remarkable feature is the use of the strong opening theme as a kind of rondo-subject, which reappears (always with "Beatus vir qui timet Dominum" as the text) several times before yielding finally to a much more solemn and chordal statement that prepares the way for the "Gloria Patri":

Ex. 34

*Laudate Dominum I* (xv, 481),[18] although scored for precisely the same combination as this *Beatus vir,* would not so appear if one were to judge by the printed editions thus far available. The parts designated "Alto I" and "Basso II" are quite superfluous. The former derives from an extra tenor part printed in error by Magni, and subsequently reprinted an octave higher in modern editions, while the latter is a ripieno bass part whose music is doubled by Bass I, functioning for both solo and tutti lines. It is worthy of note that in a composition whose main choral texture is SSATTB, Monteverdi usually restricts his solo parts to SSTTB, omitting the alto altogether. Nevertheless, after introducing a new motive into the solo parts, he is not averse to restating his case in a more sonorous fashion with the aid of the full choir:

18. Eulenburg miniature score, edited by D. Arnold (London, 1966).

[89]

Ex. 35

The hymns for vespers are set out in an original and pragmatic manner. Considerable choice is offered to the user: one, two, or three voices; four distinct musical settings; three different metrical schemes. But these are presented in such a way that they overlap, and in consequence texts in notably divergent meters can easily be adapted to identical music — as with *Deus tuorum* (xv, 614) in 8.8.8.8., and *Iste Confessor* (xv, 618) in 11.11.11. 5. On the other hand, texts in one and the same meter can be applied to totally different music — as with the two settings of *Sanctorum meritis* (xv, 606 and 610). The schema is as follows:

| Title | Voice | Metre | Feast | Setting |
|---|---|---|---|---|
| Sanctorum meritis | S | 12.12.12.8 | Common of Martyrs | 1 |
| Sanctorum meritis | T | " | " " | |
| Deus tuorum militum[19] | T | 8.8.8.8. | Common, One Martyr | 2 |
| Iste Confessor | T | 11.11.11.5 | Confessor Bishop | |
| Iste Confessor | SS | " | " " | |
| Ut queant laxis | SS | " | Nativity St. John Baptist | 3 |
| Deus tuorum militum | TTB | 8.8.8.8. | Common, One Martyr | 4 |

19. Also for St Stephen.

It should be understood that these all form part of a long tradition of alternating hymns, and accordingly only the first, third, and fifth verses are printed in the *Selva*. There is no question of interpolating the even-numbered verses in chant, unless a strange mixture of styles is to be tolerated and (in some cases) a break in the flow of music. In all probability these missing verses were recited *submissa voce* during the ritornels.

To the hymns of the *Selva* should be added one from 1651, *En gratulemur hodie* (xvi, 517), which resembles the larger group by reason of its scoring for two violins and continuo. The solo tenor is given verses 1, 3, and 5 of a seven-verse hymn in honor of St. Anthony of Padua,[20] whose altar is naturally one of the most important in S. Maria Gloriosa dei Frari. The hymn may well have been written for vespers of St. Anthony, but the published version replaces his name with "N," and the reference to St. Francis at the beginning of the second verse does not appear, since the even-numbered verses are missing. It could therefore have been sung in honor of any saint, but the notation proves that Monteverdi had the great Franciscan doctor and confessor in mind:

Ex. 36

in cu- ius au - la     glo     -          ri - a     iam iu- bi- let [An - to - ni - us]

The hymns could of course be used either with the large-scale and more opulently scored psalms, or with the others. But in the case of the two Manificat settings, there is a clear distinction, although both share the same tone (1D). The *Magnificat a 4* (xv, 703) provides polyphony for only the odd-numbered verses, its general style being

20. *Analecta Hymnica* IV, p. 90.

suffused with a restrained lyricism suitable at the same time for the text of the canticle and the modest resources required. Its plainsong verses, unlike those of the hymns, constitute an essential part of any performance.[21] The larger *Magnificat* (xv, 639) was unfortunately published without the alto and bass part of the second choir, although they can both be supplied with little difficulty —the former from the harmonic context and the latter from the continuo bass line.[22] Unusually for Monteverdi, the viola part is fully written out and lends an air of richness and solemnity to the tutti sections. The opening bars, instead of stating the psalm tone, refer back to the concluding motive of an antiphon, and in view of Monteverdi's duties in regard to Christmas music at St. Mark's,[23] or to the elaborate services on the Feast of the Ascension,[24] it might have been *Hodie Christus natus est* or *O Rex gloriae*, both of which end with an "alleluia" identical with the opening motive of the Magnificat:

A masterpiece of contrasting color and subtle symmetry, this composition of Monteverdi's maturity proves how closely he looked at even the most familiar of texts. One of his boldest and most successful strokes is the organization of the sixth, seventh, and eighth verses into a central complex of pillars by unleashing "Fecit potentiam" three

21. Nevertheless it has been recorded without them; and the double-choir Magnificat has been recorded more than once with two voice-parts missing, which turns the bass duet into a bass solo. The latter work is discussed in Stevens, 'Wagner vs. Monteverdi', *American Choral Review* 12 (1970): 95.

22. See the edition by Denis Stevens and John Steele (London: Novello, 1969).

23. Letters dated December 29, 1616, and October 30, 1627.

24. Letter dated April 21, 1618.

times as an energy-charged choral ritornel. Each statement leads to a duet for soloists, repeating the verbal and musical themes and then going on to new material. Sopranos praise God's scattering of the proud, basses sing of the mighty brought low, and lastly, tenors tell of the hungry being filled with good things. The two choirs, used less for antiphonal effects than for contrasts between heavy homophony and intricate pattern-weaving, serve as twin buttresses all the way along this elaborate and finely balanced musical structure, which repays the closest study and attention.

# 14
# *Compline*

Although Monteverdi did not set the proper psalms of Compline (which were rarely sung in polyphony), he left no fewer than five versions of the antiphon, *Salve Regina,* traditionally sung before the altar of the Blessed Virgin from Trinity until Advent, at the end of that service. Into these delicate compositions, full of a tender virtuosity so quintessentially Monteverdian, he has poured a wealth of musical thought and reverence that may even suggest, to some listeners, the soft light of waxed tapers glowing in honor of the Five Joys of Mary. There are two solo versions, two duets, and a trio, all with basso continuo only—except for the troped *Salve Regina I* (xv, 724) in which violins are added.

This remarkable work begins not with the words of the antiphon but with "Audi, caelum, verba mea," a poem on the Virgin written in such a way that the final word of each verse can be truncated and "echoed" by another voice: *gaudio* becomes *audio; benedicam* is shortened to *dicam*, to give but two examples. The complete text was set as a duet (with choral finale) in the collection of 1610,[1] but in the *Selva* Monteverdi uses only the first two-thirds, down to "pro culpis remedium," which corresponds to the cadence before the chorus entry in the earlier setting. It is worthy of note that the violins play only when the antiphon text occurs, whereas the basso continuo suffices for the trope. Some idea of the interaction of the two textual elements may be gained from the following sample:[2]

| *Trope* | *Antiphon* | *Scoring* |
|---|---|---|
| Maria Virgo illa dulcis predicata a prophetis, Ezechiel porta orientalis? | | T.1. & B.c. |
| Talis. | | T.2 & B.c. |
| O Maria, | [Salve Regina,] mater misericordiae: Vita, dulcedo, et spes nostra, salve. | T.1, 2 vns & B.c. |
| Illa sacra et felix porta per quam mors fuit expulsa introducta autem vita? | | T.1 & B.c. |
| Ita. | | T.2 & B.c. |
| O felix porta, | ad te clamamus, exsules, filii Hevae. Ad te suspiramus, gementes et flentes in hac lacrimarum valle. | T.1, 2 vns & B.c. |

1. See chap. 15.
2. Tropes to the *Salve Regina* were especially popular during the fifteenth century, as may be seen in the settings by H. de Salinis and John Dunstable. Monteverdi's trope is briefly discussed by Bettina Lupo, "Sacre monodie monteverdiane," *Musica* 2 (1943): 70 ff.

The echo tenor, necesssarily limited to the declaiming of isolated words, nevertheless needs an unusually sharp sense of synchronization if he is to coincide perfectly with a passage such as this one, which follows the last quotation above:

Ex. 38

In *Salve Regina II* (xv, 736) the two tenors enjoy a more equal allocation of words and music. The parallelism within the text suggests exchanges between the voice parts, yet there are splendid sections in which they combine in delicate chains of thirds. With alto, tenor, and bass sharing the antiphon in *Salve Regina III* (xv, 741) a new way has to be found in order to ensure balance and proportion, but Monteverdi achieves this almost effortlessly by treating the work as a kind of dialogue, especially at "Eia ergo, advocata nostra" and "ostende, O clemens."

*Salve Regina IV* (xvi, 475) was published in Calvo's anthology of 1624 as a virtuoso work for solo tenor. The unexpected opening, in the manner of a prelude, draws upon the final words of the antiphon as a kind of ecstatic invocation, and this is followed at once by a magnificent cadenza, a simplified version of which occurs later on:[3]

Ex. 39

The cadenza having come to an end, the antiphon text begins, but Monteverdi cannot refrain from recalling his prelude (now in a fervent tripla) and inserting it, trope-like, into the liturgical text. An apparently straightforward setting, *Salve Regina V* (xvi, 502) introduces a mini-trope ("Ad te clamamus [O Regina], ad te suspiramus"), omitting the words *exsules, filii Hevae.* Monteverdi's awareness of the liberty he took is apparent in the brilliant *ribattuto della gola* and *trillo* that occur at this particular point.

3. Monteverdi may possibly have wanted the singer to ornament the passage as before, and therefore wrote out the repeat in skeletal form.

# 15
# *Motets*

Inevitably, the firstfruits of young Monteverdi's studies in composition were dedicated to a patron in his home province, and the first motet of the *Sacrae Cantiunculae* was written especially for Dom Stefano Caninio — *Lapidabant Stephanum* (xiv, 1). Its gracious, sometimes innocent three-part counterpoint is typical of the motets in this admirable collection, which has been frequently discussed and analyzed.[1] Most of the texts can be found in the breviary, the remainder being biblical, so that performances could equally well have taken place in church or in some musical meeting or *accademia*. It so happened, however, that the composer's earliest professional contacts were in the realm of secular music, and his output of madrigals at first dwarfed his contribution to the liturgy. His Milanese friend Aquilino Coppini accordingly asked permission to replace the madrigal texts by

1. See *Istituzioni e Monumenti dell'Arte Musicale Italiana* 6:216; Schrade, *Monteverdi*, p. 86.

sacred words, knowing full well that Monteverdi had little or no time to devote to the real thing. The result was a series of three collections of *Musica tolta da i madrigali di Claudio Monteverdi . . . e fatta spirituale.*[2]

The five motets in the Marian collection of 1610 offer a wide diversity of style and texture: monody, duet, and trio all find their place alongside an *Audi caelum* (xiv, 227) that is essentially a tenor solo generously provided with eloquent and expressive fioriture, assisted by an echo tenor and a six-part chorus at the very end. The *Sonata sopra Sancta Maria* (xiv, 250), repeats a brief invocation from the Litany of Loreto over a richly scored orchestral sonata whose course is enlivened with changes of meter and instrumentation.[3]

In 1615 Monteverdi made his first contribution to an important anthology, the *Parnassus musicus Ferdinandaeus* of Bonometti.[4] As its title implies, it was dedicated to the Archduke Ferdinand at Graz, where the court chapel maintained a traditional welcome for Italian musicians. Although Monteverdi's artistic relationship with the Habsburgs does not become clear until 1638, this early invitation may have been extended as a result of the Salzburg performance of his *Orfeo* in 1614.[5] Either sopranos or tenors are specified for *Cantate Domino* (xvi, 409), the opening motive serving as a rondo-subject that alternates with episodes in contrasting meter and frequently provided with brilliant ornamentation. The duetting voices are closely integrated thematically as they

---

2. Complete list in Arnold, *Monteverdi*, pp. 192-95. The complete set of partbooks in Milan were destroyed during World War II.

3. Other settings of *Sancta Maria* are to be found, in comparable form, among the words of Crotti, Lappi, and Franzoni.

4. See H. Federhofer, "Graz Court Musicians and their contribution to the *Parnassus Musicus Ferdinandaeus*," *Musica Disciplina* 9 (1955):167.

5. Theophil Antonicek, "Claudio Monteverdi und Österreich," *Österreichische Musikzeitschrift* 26 (1971):267.

weave patterns from Psalm 97 (verses 1, 2, 3, and 5). Five years later, and for six voices, another *Cantate Domino* (xvi, 422) relies on a different selection of verses, in spite of the similarity of incipit—Psalms 95 (1,2) and 97 (1,5,6). This extroverted setting of a joyful text recalls a melodic phrase from *Ecco mormorar l'onde*:[6]

Ex. 40 (a)

(b)

This motet is found in a collection by one of Monteverdi's friends in Cremona, the cornetto player Giulio Cesare Bianchi. Also included are two motets possibly referred to obliquely in a letter of 1618,[7] concerning the preparations

6. First pointed out by D. Arnold, "Formal Design in Monteverdi's Church Music," *C.M. e il suo tempo*, pp. 189-90.
7. April 21, 1618—"il giorno di Santa Croce" (first motet: "quia per Sanctam Crucem tuam") "si esponserà il Santissimo Sangue" (second motet: "quia per sanguinem tuum pretiosum").

for the feast of the Finding of the Holy Cross — *Christe adoramus te* (xvi, 428) and *Adoramus te Christe* (xvi, 439). Bianchi brought out a second book in the same year, introducing for the first time Monteverdi's six-part *Litany of the B.V.M.* (xvi, 382), which was reprinted by Calvo in 1626 and again in the posthumously published volume of 1650. This fine setting, which makes considerable use of dialogue, belongs to a class of Litanies of the Rosary often to be found among the works of sixteenth-century composers.[8]

Yet another anthology of 1620, Calvo's *Symbolae diversorum musicorum*, offers motets on St. John the Baptist, *Fugge anima mea* (xvi, 444), and on St. Roche, *O beatae viae* (xvi, 454). Both are duets, the first indulging from time to time in alternating solos accompanied by an obbligato violin that never plays in the tutti sections. Perhaps each singer doubled on the violin, after the fashion of the musicians at the Scuola di San Rocco described by Thomas Coryate: "those that played upon the treble viols, sung and played together."[9]

A letter dated March 26, 1611, offers Duke Vincenzo "a little motet for the Elevation" (a 2) and another for the Virgin (a 5). Nothing fits the description of the first-mentioned until 1622, when Donfrid issued the two-part setting of *O bone Jesu* (xvi, 506) — a simple but moving version of a favorite text, which appears in many different forms throughout the Renaissance.[10] Another possibility is *Venite sitientes ad acquas Domini* (xvi, 467), published with two more Monteverdi motets by Lorenzo Calvo in 1624. In the following year, Sammaruco's *Sacri Affetti* features a motet for an unusual combination of voices,

8. Giovanni Gabrieli, *Collected Works,* ed. D. Arnold, 3:109; Palestrina, *Collected Works* (Breitkopf), 26 passim.
9. Thomas Coryate, *Crudities* (London, 1905), p. 389.
10. See Robert Carver, *Omnia Opera,* ed. Denis Stevens, vol. 1, Preface.

at least as far as Monteverdi is concerned: *Ego dormio* (xvi, 481) for soprano and bass. Although the text (from the *Song of Songs*) could hardly be described as a dialogue, it is cheerfully and effectively transformed into one, with no loss of prestige or purpose.

Of the four motets published by Simonetti in 1625, one is apparently unique as regards its text, which is a prose commentary on the Eucharist: *Ecce sacrum paratum* (xvi, 497). The solo tenor part is devoid of embellishment (which does not mean that something appropriate might not have been added) and the declamation is perfectly plain and straightforward. *Currite populi* (xvi, 491) appeals at once by reason of its rising sequential theme in jubilant tripla measure. This reappears several times as a frame for contrasting arioso sections, the text being in honor of any saint. The saint's name can be inserted after the words *celebremus diem festum*. . . .

*Sancta Maria, succurre miseris* (xvi, 511), for two sopranos, is the Magnificat antiphon at first vespers of the Feast of Our Lady of Mount Carmel. Published in 1627 by Donfrid, its shadow flits across a letter dated July 24 of the same year, when Monteverdi mentions his involvement with the music at the Carmelite Church in Venice for that very feast. In view of this unusual coincidence, it could be assumed that the motet was first performed on that particular evening, under the composer's direction. Calvo's collection of 1629 included a virtuosic monody based on the text *Exulta filia Sion*,[11] and a five-voice motet— *Exultent caeli*[12]—which is a strong candidate for the "motet in honor of the Virgin" mentioned in the letter of 1611 discussed above. It was by no means unusual for Monteverdi to delay publication, even for ten or twenty years.

11. Osthoff, *12 Compositioni Vocali*, p. 32.
12. Ibid., p. 39.

Since the *Selva morale* is mainly given over to masses, psalms, and hymns, there is little room for motets as such, but the few included are not without distinction. *Ab aeterno ordinata sum* (xv, 189) must surely rank as the most splendid of all Monteverdi's bass solos, written perhaps for his old friend and colleague G. B. Marinoni. If its descriptive passages verge on the spectacular, so too does the range needed for its performance:

Ex. 41
Bass

*Jubilet tota civitas* (xv, 748), whose text could refer to any martyr,[13] is unusual in that the forces required for performance are larger than they appear to be. It is for "one voice in dialogue," which may mean a solo set against all the others in unison. *Iam moriar* (xv, 757) is a not unworthy contrafactum of Ariadne's lament, while *Laudate Dominum* (xv, 753) counts as Monteverdi's only surviving setting of Psalm 150. The motet (also a monody) with the same incipit in 1650 is a setting of Psalm 116, and it is worth noting that its heady ornamentation (xvi, 227) does not appear in the same generous fashion in Casati's reprint of the following year (xv, 519).

13. The phrase "Iste sanctus pro lege Dei sui certavit usque ad mortem" in vespers of a martyr is clearly the origin of the slightly longer phrase in the motet: "Quis est iste sanctus qui pro lege Dei tam illustri vita et insignis operationibus usque ad mortem operatus ets?" The suggestion that this motet is in honor of St. Benedict is hereby withdrawn (see my article "C.M.: Selva morale e spirituale," *C.M. e il suo tempo*, p. 432).

# III
# MUSIC FOR THE STAGE

# 16

# *Introduction*

In the process of offering Striggio, with as much impartiality as might be expected from a rival, his considered opinion of the Cremonese organist, composer, and instrument-maker Galeazzo Sirena, Monteverdi stressed the point that a composer steeped in the ecclesiastical style would have no small difficulty in coping with the complexities of theater music — unless of course he had prior experience in this area. At the time of writing that letter (September 10, 1609) Monteverdi could claim to have had a close association with stage music for some twenty years,[1] and it is safe to assume that he knew what he was talking about. He continued to be involved with the baroque theater, in all its strange and fascinating aspects, until the year before he died. Yet the greater part of this not inconsiderable

---

1. On arriving at Mantua in 1589, Monteverdi would have been involved without delay in the Gonzagas' continual round of theatrical entertainments. He might even have witnessed, or taken part in, the Florentine intermezzi for *La Pellegrina* of that very year, when two Mantuan musicians were loaned especially for this occasion. See D. P. Walker, *Les Fêtes de Florence* (Paris, 1963), 1:xli.

portion of his total output seems to be irretrievably lost. In the following list, titles of lost works are given in italics. Dates refer to the premiere (when the year is known) or to the first documentary mention. A few compositions still elude these chronological nets, and their dates (marked *) therefore denote year of publication.

| DATE | TITLE | LIBRETTIST |
|------|-------|------------|
| 1595 | Il Pastor Fido (pastoral drama) | Guarini |
| 1604 | [Endimione] (ballet) | ? |
| 1607 | Orfeo (favola in musica) | Striggio |
| 1607* | De la bellezza le dovute lodi (ballet) | ? |
| 1608 | Arianna (opera — Lament only survives) | Rinuccini |
| 1608 | Il Ballo delle Ingrate (opera-ballet) | Rinuccini |
| 1608 | Prologue to L'Idropica (commedia by Guarini) | Chiabrera |
| 1616 | Tirsi e Clori (ballet) | ? |
| 1616 | Le Nozze di Tetide (intermezzi) | Agnelli |
| 1617 | Prologue to La Maddalena (sacred drama) | G. B. Andreini |
| 1618 | Adromeda (intermezzi ?) | Marigliani |
| 1619* | Lettera amorosa; Partenza amorosa (rappresentativo) | Achillini |
| 1620 | Apollo (rappresentativo?) | Striggio |
| 1622 | Le contese dei duoi amori (intermezzi for Le Tre Costanti) | Marigliani |
| 1624 | Combattimento di Tancredi e Clorinda (rappresentativo) | Tasso |
| 1627 | [Armida] (rappresentativo) | Tasso |
| 1627 | La finta pazza Licori | Strozzi |
| 1628 | Prologue to Aminta (drama by Tasso) | Achillini |
| 1628 | Intermezzi for Tasso's Aminta | Ascanio Pio |
| 1628 | Mercurio e Marte (torneo) | Achillini |
| 1630 | Proserpina rapita (opera) | Strozzi |
| 1636 | Movete al mio bel suon (ballet) | Rinuccini |
| 1638* | Lamento della ninfa (rappresentativo) | Rinuccini |
| 1639 | Adone (opera) | Vendramin |

| 1640 | Il Ritorno d'Ulisse in Patria (opera) | Badoaro |
| 1641 | Le Nozze d'Enea con Lavinia (opera) | Badoaro |
| 1641 | La Vittoria d'Amore (ballet) | Morando |
| 1642 | L'Incoronazione di Poppea (opera) | Busenello |

Most of this music falls naturally into one of the accepted categories of theatrical entertainment—opera, ballet, intermezzo, and torneo. A few compositions, though they do not defy pigeonholing, could fit into two or more places, depending upon the whim of the modern interpreter of history or of music. The *Combattimento*, for example, loses nothing of its power when given in the concert hall as if it were a secular oratorio; on the other hand, success often attends a well-produced ballet, and it was after all recommended by Monteverdi as a composition "in genere rappresentativo." By this he clearly meant that the work could be performed on a stage, but he did not imply that a chamber-music rendering would be out of the question.

# 17

# *In Genere Rappresentativo*

It is in many ways typical of Monteverdi that he made almost immediate use of his *Pastor Fido* settings as madrigals. Stage productions were rare and expensive — the dazzling reflections of princely pleasures that the world at large could never hope to imitate or reproduce. Guarini's pastoral had been the first choice of Duke Vincenzo's favorite lady, Agnese del Carretto (later Marchioness of Grana), and it was no mere coincidence that the child born of their attachment was named Silvio, after one of the characters in the play. But the production took seven or eight years to take shape, spelling frustration for all but the most patient of composers and actors.[1] And even when success finally came, the music would have remained totally unknown had not the printer lent his powerful aid, thanks to which Monteverdi's

1. For a detailed discussion of the music for *Il Pastor Fido*, see A. Cavicchi, "Teatro monteverdiano e tradizione teatrale ferrarese," *Claudio Monteverdi e il suo tempo* (Verona, 1969), p. 139.

contributions to the Ferrarese and Mantuan productions appeared with the minimum of delay in his fourth and fifth books of madrigals.[2] They were not at this stage given the subtitle "in genere rappresentativo" because the term was unknown and undiscovered—indeed, it did not appear until Book VII. But the intention was clear enough: the music could be sung as a sequence of madrigals, or (for those sufficiently wealthy) it could quickly and easily be restored to its pristine function as the vital musical element in a drama.

Sacred drama too made occasional demands on Monteverdi, as when his friend G. B. Andreini, father of Virginia (who had sung the part of Ariadne in 1608), invited him to compose a prologue for *La Maddalena* (xi, 170), performed in Mantua in 1617. Three other musicians also contributed to the score, which was published in Venice in the same year. Monteverdi's share, although modest in scope, served to keep his name before the Mantuan court audiences. Three years later, when Caterina Medici Gonzaga received her specially bound dedicatee's copy of Book VII, she would have noticed two familiar "letter scenes" intended for stage presentation— monodies for soprano and tenor respectively, if credence is given to the clefs, which made G. B. Doni complain about Monteverdi's lack of regard for the meaning of the text.[3] The *Lettera amorosa* (vii, 160), which sets to music a poem by Claudio Achillini (with whom Monteverdi was later to collaborate in the entertainments for Parma[4]) sounds much more convincing when sung by a tenor—the designated voice for the *Partenza amorosa* (vii, 167)—

2. See chap. 2.

3. *Lyra Barberina* (Florence, 1763), App. p. 26.

4. The attribution was first made known by C. Gallico, "La 'Lettera amorosa' di Monteverdi," *Nuova Rivista Musicale Italiana* 1 (1967):287.

and it should be remembered that clefs in monodies were then freely interchangeable.

*Apollo*, described in Monteverdi's correspondence as an eclogue "con gesto," clearly belongs to the representative style, and in view of the success accorded to a Venetian performance of the Lamenti,[5] its total loss is regrettable. Nevertheless, the various ideals associated with favola, intermezzo, and ballet were being replaced by new thoughts, inspired by Monteverdi's reading of Plato and Boethius. Whether or not he interpreted correctly all that he read is a matter for conjecture. What remains is the summary of his findings in the preface to Book VIII,[6] and the music composed in accordance with those new-found principles. Their first impact on the public, at the performance of the *Combattimento di Tancredi e Clorinda* (viii, 132),[7] seems to have been considerable, and it would be tempting to search for contemporaneous accounts of that remarkable evening at the Palazzo Mocenigo during the carnival season of 1624.

The *Combattimento* is a far cry from the Tasso settings in Book III. Instead of a five-part polyphonic texture, there is one single, vital line sung by the narrator, whose task consists not only of telling the story but of illustrating the tempo of events and the subtleties of language. The voices of Tancredi and Clorinda are heard only in brief exchanges and occasional solos. Just as in certain kinds of romantic opera the drama unfolds in the orchestra, so Monteverdi's strings and harpsichord provide much of the tension and relaxation in this passionate episode from *La Gerusalemme Liberata*. If at times the harpsichord

---

5. See in particular the letters dated January 9 and February 1, 1620. Other sections of the work are mentioned in subsequent letters in that year.
6. Oliver Strunk, trans., *Source Readings in Music History* (New York, 1950), p. 413.
7. A fully collated text, with preface and translation, may be seen in the practical edition published by Oxford University Press (London, 1962).

outgrows its basic function in order to suggest the jangling of heavy armor, its silence when Clorinda is vanquished also ranks as a dramatic eloquence:

Ex. 42

The emotional drive of this work, requiring a minimum of eight musicians and scarcely more than twenty minutes to perform, seems out of all proportion to its physical properties. Schütz, on his second visit to Venice in 1628, was so impressed that he attempted a German version.[8] Since the work was then unpublished, he might perhaps have heard a performance under the composer's direction, with a narrator who added the necessary ornaments to the stanza beginning 'Notte, che nel profondo oscuro seno. . . .'"[9]

The man upon whom the *Combattimento* made its deepest impression was Monteverdi. His audience reacted in exactly the way he knew they would, for his rediscovery of bellicose rhythmic patterns made hearts beat faster just as the systaltic ethos forced tears from the glassiest of eyes. What was more logical than a parergon, whose text should also come from Tasso's *La Gerusalemme Liberata*?

8. W. Osthoff, "Monteverdis Combattimento in deutscher Sprache und Heinrich Schütz," *Festschrift Helmuth Osthoff zum 65. Geburtstage* (Tutzing, 1961), p. 195.
9. The kind of ornamentation required is discussed and suggested in the O.U.P. edition.

On May 1, 1627 (just over three years after the premiere of the *Combattimento*) there is a reference to a setting of "many stanzas from Tasso, where Armida begins 'O tu che porte / parte teco di me, parte ne lassi,'[10] continuing with the entire lament and anger, with Rinaldo's reply." This episode runs to a dozen stanzas—in other words, it was a composition of about the same length as the *Combattimento*—and was probably scored for the same resources. Two further letters of 1627 mention the work as *Armida*, and on February 4, 1628, the composer remembers that his copy is at Mocenigo's house[11]—the patron and place so closely connected with the path-breaking performance of 1624. The original manuscript therefore remained in Venice, and a copy was made for Striggio in Mantua. Neither seems to have survived.

In the *Lament of the Nymph* (viii, 286) two friends— composer and poet, Cremonese and Florentine—collaborated in the creation of a rare gem, albeit a miniature one. The poem had been set before,[12] but in Monteverdi's hands it took on a new meaning and intensity. The forlorn girl steps forth slowly from her dwelling, while three sympathetic souls commiserate with her in heart-rending harmonies; on reaching center stage she begins to lament the loss of her lover. The *chaconne* bass, with its built-in V-I cadence at each repeat, provides subliminal sadness and structural strength, yet its very punctuation

10. Pirrotta and Barblan, among others, have erroneously censured Monteverdi for misquoting these lines. The spelling errors should be attributed to the anonymous transcriber(s) of the Malipiero edition of the letters (Milan, 1929). The composer's one forgivable lapse is the transposition of two words: *teco parte*.

11. Formerly the Palazzo Dandolo, acquired and refurbished by Mocenigo in 1620. This building is now the Hotel Danieli.

12. By Antonio Brunelli in his *Scherzi, Arie, Canzonette e Madrigali* of 1614. Modern edition in Putnam Aldrich, *Rhythm in Seventeenth-Century Italian Monody* (New York, 1966), p. 166.

is a challenge to the composer, and he meets the challenge and modifies the punctuation with unerring skill:

Ex. 43

# 18
# Ballets

Of Monteverdi's six known ballet scores, the first and last
have been lost, but the four that remain speak eloquently
for his strong affinity with this still rather unfamiliar aspect
of courtly entertainment. Mantua nourished a strong
tradition of dancing, and her masters of that art were
among the best in Italy.[1] Writing from Cremona to Duke
Vincenzo in December 1604, Monteverdi sends ballet
music for a scene featuring shepherds and stars, apparently
part of a work about the moongod Endymion.[2] He goes
into some detail about the alternating scheme he has
devised, playing off stringed instruments against other
groups, but says that he cannot complete one of the sections
until he knows the exact number of dancers. This ballet,

1. See the entries for Balli e Ballerini in A. Bertolotti, *Musici alla Corte dei Gonzaga
in Mantova* (Milan, 1890), p. 121.
2. Duke Ferdinando devised a *favola* about Endymion for his own wedding entertainments in 1617; Ademollo, *La Bell'Adriana* (Città di Castello, 1888), p. 232. The same
character is mentioned in a letter of Monteverdi to the Marquis Bentivoglio dated
September 10, 1617 (*recte* 1627).

whose title could have been *Endimione*, was doubtless intended for the carnival of 1605, but Federico Zuccari, who was in Mantua at that time, makes no mention of it. He does, however, describe the reverberant acoustics of the Palazzo del Te, and the effect they had on music performed there.[3]

An early example of an "entrata and ballet," comparable perhaps to the one mentioned in Monteverdi's letter to the duke, may be seen in *De la bellezza le dovute lodi* (x, 62), published as the final number of the *Scherzi* of 1607. Doubt has sometimes been cast on the authorship of this work, perhaps because it follows two scherzi by the composer's younger brother, Giulio Cesare. But there are plentiful examples of the best and most typical of Claudian cadences, and he even borrows a phrase from one of his own scherzi:

Ex. 44

The often rapid alternation of instrumental and vocal passages in the body of this ballet agrees quite closely with Monteverdi's known predilections, and the work as a whole may be considered as a fair specimen of his Mantuan dance music. Only a decade later his ideas took on a bolder and more symphonic shape in the ballet *Tirsi e Clori*. But his next extant ballet was embedded in a predominant-

3. Quoted in Ademollo, p. 52. See also Doni's remarks about acoustics in Mantua in *Lyra Barberina*, 2:171.

ly vocal work—*Il Ballo delle Ingrate* (viii, 314)[4]—composed for the marriage of Francesco Gonzaga and Margherita of Savoy. It so happened that Monteverdi's ballet, based on a text by Rinuccini, was not the only one of its kind to be performed at those festivities. The bridegroom himself devised a "balletto," *Il Sacrificio d'Ifigenia*, concerning which Striggio explained to him (April 27, 1608) that extra scenes were being added secretly to the rival spectacle in order to ensure its supremacy.[5] Although Striggio betrays his personal anxiety, some stimulus could have come from the Duchess Eleonora, who—not content with chastising those responsible for the overall plan of events—even went so far as to criticize the poets and musicians themselves.

*Il Ballo delle Ingrate* enjoyed a well-deserved success, if one can believe the comments of ambassadors and connoisseurs, for in spite of the scarcely veiled commendation of amorous intrigue implicit in the libretto (which must have appealed to Vincenzo, who danced as a member of the troupe, along with his son Francesco) it was resurrected some thirty years later for a performance at the much straiter-laced Imperial court in Vienna and then published as part of Book VIII. On this occasion, the references to Mantua were replaced by suitable words and phrases expressive of the new locale, such as *Istro* (Danube) instead of *Manto*. There is no reason to suppose that the music was in any way refurbished, for the printed libretto of 1608 remains virtually unchanged in the edition of 1638, so that the only additions and subtractions would have occurred in the purely instrumental part of the score.[6]

4. For a practical version giving full five-part harmony for the central ballet, see Schott Edition 10715 (London, 1960).
5. Canal, *Della Musica in Mantova* (Venice, 1881), p. 83.
6. A. A. Abert assumes however that there was some reworking of musical material. See *Claudio Monteverdi und das musikalische Drama* (Lippstadt, 1954), p. 33.

The central ballet is still occasionally performed in modern revivals as if it were scored for string quartet, even though the harmony sounds depressingly dull and the absence of five-part string writing — a special feature of ballet music in the French style — should arouse suspicion. The restoration of the overlooked second violin part adds both sonority and harmonic spice to the texture:

Ex. 45

Monteverdi's experiments with simultaneous false relations had yielded, by this time, the kind of result that served to intensify to a remarkable degree that latent emotion of a farewell such as was sung by Virginia Andreini during the final scene, when the frigid ladies return to Hell, their cold hearts to be warmed by fires other than those of love.

The progression of each voice part is logical and musical;
the harmony that blossoms forth is sheer magic:

Ex. 46

*Tirsi e Clori* (vii, 191),[7] a ballet of a simple and
straightforward kind, is described in a letter of the
composer to Iberti,[8] dated November 21, 1615. The two
main characters sing in dialogue to their own accompaniment, backed up by continuo instruments in the orchestra—a theorbo for Chloris, and a harpsichord for Thyrsis.
When the reluctance of the lady has been overcome and
she is ready to join in the dance, they sing a duet that
leads to a choral "riverenza" and the beginning of the
ballet proper. The various changes of measure and melody
then ensue, with instruments doubling the voices where
necessary or desirable, until a final solemn bow brings the
work to a close.

7. For a practical edition with preface and translation, see the Penn State Music
Series, No. 14, edited by Kenneth Cooper.
8. Not, as usually stated, to Striggio (who was then in Milan). Further evidence of
Iberti's interest in this ballet may be seen in Camillo Sordi's letter to him, also dated
November 21, in the Archivio Gonzaga (Busta 1547, E xlv, no. 3).

In the ballet *Movete al mio bel suon* (viii, 157),[9] instrumental parts are written out in full, even though the texture is no more elaborate than that of a trio sonata — which does not prevent doubling of the violin and bass parts according to the size of the hall. Its appearance as the final item of the warlike madrigals in Book VIII, and its frequent and flattering references to the Emperor Ferdinand III (to whom the volume is dedicated), would seem to leave no doubt about the purpose of the libretto, but in fact it turns out to be a reworking of a much earlier poem by one of Monteverdi's oldest friends. The composer, casting about for a suitable text for his ballet — probably performed on December 30, 1636, for the imperial coronation — found a pair of sonnets in praise of Henry IV of France in a volume of Rinuccini's poetry published in Florence in 1622.[10] By changing all the topical and personal references, and by inverting the order of the sonnets, Monteverdi succeeded in fabricating an "occasional" poem whose origin was certainly never guessed by those who heard the performance.

As in *Tirsi e Clori*, there is an introductory section dominated by monody. A singer, dressed as a poet, comes forward and invokes peace and plenty, his arioso quatrains framed by lively ritornels. He calls upon a nymph to present the lyre and the laurel, so that he may tell of the glorious deeds of a new king. His plea to the dancers that they move their nimble feet to the sounds of his music sets the ballet on its way, and at this point a five-part chorus enters and begins the second of the two sonnets. The brilliant and effective writing for voices tends to follow the

9. Practical version, with preface and translation, published by Faber Music (London, 1967).
10. Discovered by Nino Pirrotta. See *Scelte poetiche di Monteverdi*, p. 56.

trio-sonata idea at certain points, as when graceful roulades conjure up an image of blond and flowing tresses:

At the end of part one, a "canario" or a "passamezzo" is played while the singers rest, after which, returning to the same musical motive that began the ballet, the chorus launches once more into a fanfare in honor of the king's military prowess.

A libretto, but (alas) no music, survives from Monteverdi's last ballet, *La Vittoria d'Amore*.[11] Commissioned in 1641 by Odoardo Farnese, for whom the festival music of 1628 had been written, it was intended to celebrate the birth of a prince. Bernardo Morandi wrote the poem, and the ballet was performed with appropriately ingenious

11. Discussed by A. Solerti in "Un balletto musicato da Claudio Monteverde, *"Rivista musicale italiana"* 11 (1904):24.

pieces of stage machinery in the citadel of Piacenza, where the duke preferred to spend the carnival season. Thus ended Monteverdi's thirty-seven years of close association with the art of the ballet.

# 19
# Intermezzi and Tornei

Since the Renaissance intermezzo, like the medieval trope, appears to have been designed purely and simply in order to extend what was already quite lengthy, it is therefore difficult to explain or justify its function in terms of present-day theatrical conventions. But whereas the trope served as a gloss or commentary on an existing text, sometimes turning it gently in another direction, the intermezzo often set out to provide contrast to the main play into which it was inserted. Its purpose was to distract rather than to consolidate. Nevertheless, its extraordinary and often bizarre combination of acting, singing, dancing, and elaborate stage machinery exerted over the majority of the audience a kind of irresistible artistic attraction, in spite of the fact that they had to endure six or seven hours of dubiously comfortable accommodation.

Guarini's prose comedy *L'Idropica,* already a well-proportioned entertainment demanding some four hours of unremitting concentration, was extended to seven hours for the performance in June 1608 by the simple expedient of commissioning Chiabrera to write a Prologue, four intermezzi, and a licenza, these six new elements framing the five acts of the original play. Monteverdi, always attracted by Chiabrera's poetry, much of which he set in the *Scherzi* of 1607, agreed to provide the music for the Prologue, and others among the court musicians took care of the rest. The music is lost—true, unfortunately, of all Monteverdi's intermezzi and tornei—but we know from Follino's description[1] that it must have consisted mainly of monody, for one of the great attractions was the appearance of Manto, the river goddess, daughter of the prophet Tiresias, singing delicately to the accompaniment of various instruments placed behind the stage.

If we can believe Monteverdi, it was hard at times to distinguish (from the text alone) between an opera and an intermezzo. On his return to Mantua from Milan, Striggio commissioned Monteverdi to write music for a maritime fable—*Le Nozze di Tetide*—by Count Scipione Agnelli, a better historian than he was a poet. Sensing this at once, the composer wrote back (December 9, 1616) complaining that the music for the sea gods would have to emerge from below the stage, causing the singers to force their voices; heavy wind consorts would be needed to conform with Plato's injunction "tibia [debet esse] in agris"; and many sopranos would be required for the cupids, zephyrs, and sirens. Worse still, since the whistling and howling of the winds do not rank as true speech, they would not move him in the same way as the songs of Orpheus and Ariadne.

Striggio, after consulting with Duke Ferdinando, attempted to pacify Monteverdi, who wrote again on December 29 with further ideas, including a six-part

1. A. Solerti, *Gli albori del melodramma*, 3:208.

chorus for the Argonauts and other choruses for the Nereids and Tritons. But his heart was not in this strange project, which turned out later to be a series of intermezzi with "spoken song rather than singing speech." After working hard and completing all the solo songs, he received a letter from Striggio in the second week of January saying that *Le Nozze* was to be abandoned, and his disappointed reply was sent on January 14.

Nevertheless, his correspondence reveals a keen sense of what would (and what would not) be appropriate in a stage work of this kind. He pleads for a final canzonetta, with dancing, in praise of the bridal pair; he comments on the need for contrast in the songs for the Three Sirens; and he recommends that the plaint of Peleus be sung by Adriana Basile in a loud voice, with her sisters supplying off-stage echo effects, all of this to be preceded by a sinfonia suggested by a reference in the libretto.

The Gonzagas, as is well known, frequently expected their composers to produce works of considerable dimensions in a perilously short period of time. But for once they behaved decently in this respect, when it was known that Duke Ferdinando's sister Eleonora would be married to the Emperor Ferdinand II in January 1622. Almost a year in advance, the Duchess wrote to Monteverdi inviting him to write the music for a series of intermezzi associated with Ercole Marigliani's play *Le Tre Costanti*,[2] and he replied on March 5, 1621, in a letter full of joy and gratitude. Subsequent letters to her and to Marigliani report on progress made, the third intermezzo being completed by September 10 and the licenza by November 20. The performance took place on January 18 in the

2. Davari, *Notizie biografiche,* p. 124; Solerti, *Gli albori del melodramma,* 1:120, gives full details of this work, but it has hitherto not been connected with the intermezzi upon which Monteverdi was definitely engaged at this time.

court theater at Mantua, but it is not known whether Monteverdi went there to direct the performance, which indeed he offered to do. As one might expect, the libretto was printed and survives, while the music was left in manuscript and lost.

Several recent studies of the prologue and intermezzi for Tasso's *Aminta*, and of the torneo *Mercurio e Marte*, written for the festivities at Parma on the occasion of the marriage of Odoardo Farnese and Margherita de' Medici, reveal the extent to which Monteverdi was involved as composer-in-residence and director of music.[3] Having been commissioned by the Marquis Enzo Bentivoglio early in August 1627, he wrote to him in some detail on September 10 about the third intermezzo.[4] Many subsequent letters mention Monteverdi's music, ideas, journeys, habits of composition, reactions to the theater and machinery, and a host of related matters. Everyone seems to be involved: Striggio, Bentivoglio, the Procurators of St. Mark's, the Duke Odoardo, and those in charge of arrangements in Parma—Guitti, Mazzi, and Goretti. The total impression is one of enormous artistic activity building up to two climaxes. First, the lavish production in a specially built theater in the courtyard of the church of St. Peter Martyr on December 13, 1628—*Aminta* distended by Achillini's prologue and Ascanio Pio's intermezzi;[5] and then, on December 21, in the finally

3. A. M. Nagler, *Theatre Festivals of the Medici, 1539-1637* (New Haven, Conn., 1964); I. Lavin, "Lettres de Parme (1618, 1627-28) et débuts du théâtre baroque," *Le Lieu Théâtral à la Renaissance*; S. Reiner, "Preparations in Parma—1618, 1627-28," *The Music Review* 25 (1964):273. The texts of the prologue, intermezzi, and torneo were published in Solerti, *Musica, ballo e drammatica alla Corte Medicea dal 1600 al 1637* (Florence, 1905).

4. The original letter clearly gives the date as 1617, but the events referred to seem to relate exclusively to the preparations of 1627. See Frank Walker's communication in *Music and Letters* 29 (1948):433.

5. No collective title seems to have been used for the intermezzi, but the prologue bears the name *Teti e Flora*.

inaugurated Teatro Farnese, the torneo *Mercurio e Marte*, again on a text by Achillini. Although Marcello Buttigli, the official chronicler of Parma, goes to great lengths in describing the festivities, he completely ignores the music and makes no reference to its composer. Happily, this situation is slightly improved by Luigi Inghirami (secretary to Prince Gian Carlo de' Medici), who writes about Monteverdi's wonderful music for the prologue and singles out for special praise his contribution to the third and fourth intermezzi.

The torneo, in many ways even more spectacular than the intermezzi, yet relied as much as they did on the amazing variety and quality of instrumental and vocal music. Monteverdi's prelude, played by five orchestras in widely separated positions, was only a foretaste of what was to follow. Settimia Caccini, who had already been heard as Dido in the second of the intermezzi, sang "with her angelic voice," the part of Aurora. In the next scene, madrigals were performed by groups representing key months of the four seasons. Later, Apollo and the Muses persuaded Orpheus to sing, and sing he did, causing the rocks to move, as in the old legend, until out of them (a new touch, this) sprang a squadron of knights. Settimia Caccini, now dressed as Juno, sang another splendid aria, in which she implored Berecyntia to influence Proserpina and make her set free a second group of bewitched knights. There were arias by Cupid and the amoretti, a chorus of Tritons, a solo by Neptune (the effect of which was to flood the arena with water), a licenza by Jupiter, and a concert of heavenly musicians.[6] The audience was en-

6. Nagler, *Theater Festivals*, pp. 153 ff. give a detailed account of the entire torneo. Monteverdi's earlier involvement in the music for tornei is mentioned by his brother in the *Dichiaratione*, published in 1607.

raptured—but when everything was over the music disappeared completely, as if it were nothing more than an expendable stage property.

# 20
# *Operas*

Monteverdi was forty when he wrote his first opera; his last was produced when he had reached the age of seventy-five. It would be strange indeed if there were no noticeable change of style and approach between *Orfeo* and *Poppea*, for they encompassed a period of steady but irreversible transition from private patronage to public payment, and although money was at the root of both, it was virtually unlimited in the one and tightly controlled in the other. This explains to some extent why *Orfeo*, scored for an orchestra with a great variety of instruments and choruses of different ranges, was twice published in full score, while *Poppea* requires only a small string band and such choruses as might be assembled with the aid of the principals and singers of minor roles.

The eight operas fall into a clear pattern in time, for *Orfeo* and *Arianna* belong to the composer's Mantuan period, *La finta pazza Licori* and *Proserpina rapita* to

Venice some twenty years later, and the last four follow in a yearly sequence: *Adone, Ulisse, Le nozze d'Enea, Poppea* (1639-42). Born among glittering rivalry between one court and another—Ferrara, Parma, Florence, Mantua—*L'Orfeo, favola in musica* (xi)[1] could also have been considered the outcome of an age-old family conflict, the rivalry between father and son. Since Vincenzo, fourth Duke of Mantua and Monferrato, had attained a certain notoriety as a luxury-loving spendthrift and a womanizer, his subjects were agreeably surprised to find that Francesco, his eldest son, took upon himself the role of a good man, upright and moral in his behavior, and decidedly intellectual in his leanings. He was the true patron as well as the dedicatee of *Orfeo*.

Among the vast flock of friars expelled from Venice during the interdict, there was one who—on finding refuge in Mantua in 1607—called down the wrath of God on the premiere of *Orfeo*. The theater in public was suspect enough, but in private—before a crowd of courtiers—it would surely be worse, especially when music inflamed the passions. But the performance survived, the court was enchanted, and further opportunity to hear and judge this fascinating amalgam of symphony, song, dance, and chorus was given to the ladies of the city. Francesco Rasi, the tenor who had earlier made his reputation in Peri's *Euridice* and Gagliano's *Dafne*, created the grateful but demanding title role,[2] and a boy treble named Giovanni Gualberto probably sang the prologue. All the best musicians of the court and city took part, and it was not long before the

1. Full score, with preface, translation, and critical notes published by Novello (London, 1967). See also R. Donington, "Monteverdi's First Opera," *The Monteverdi Companion* (London, 1968), p. 257.
2. See the prefatory "lettera cronologica" to Eugenio Cagnani's *Rima* of 1612, quoted in *Mantova—Le Lettere* (Mantua, 1962), 2:621.

fame of the opera and its composer spread even beyond the bounds of Italy.

The process was hastened not only by the publication of *Orfeo* in full score (Venice, 1609)[3] but also by the continuous paean of praise from listeners and critics alike. Padre Cherubino Ferrari said that "the music serves the poetry so fittingly that it cannot be replaced by anything better."[4] In Monteverdi's first extant letter to Alessandro Striggio, his librettist, he explains that on August 25 the courier from Venice should bring a copy of the printed score, which his brother Giulio Cesare will arrange to have bound and then passed to Striggio for presentation to Prince Francesco.[5] The Prince seems to have planned a performance in Turin during the following year, for he wrote from that city in January 1610 to Striggio (then at Casale Monferrato), asking for a copy to be sent at once.[6] Unhappily, this excellent relationship between prince and composer was destroyed by the jealousy of other court musicians, especially Sante Orlandi, with the result that shortly after Francesco's rise to ducal power Monteverdi and his younger brother were dismissed.

*Orfeo* succeeded because it fulfilled the ideal of a perfectly balanced artistic unity. Instrumental and vocal music are on a par, and when appropriate they join with each other to provide verses and ritornels in alternation ("Vi ricorda o boschi ombrosi" — xi, 48) or solemn choruses in true *a cappella* style ("Nulla impresa per uom" — xi, 107). The strength and personality of the main roles stand out all the more because many of the subsidiary

3. Reprinted in 1615; Facsimile edition, London, 1972.
4. Letter to Vincenzo Gonzaga, August 24, 1607.
5. Letter dated August 24, 1609.
6. Bertolotti, *Musici alla corte dei Gonzaga*, p. 92. For a performance in Salzburg see chap. 15.

parts are allowed to combine naturally in dialogue, so that the impression gained by listeners is one of contrast, flexibility, and variety. If Striggio's libretto suffers a little from stiffness, this defect is invisibly repaired by the expertise that Monteverdi brings to bear upon the delineation of character. An infallible judge of the place and purpose of a dramatic high point, he writes for Orpheus a persuasively embellished solo the likes of which had never been seen or heard before:

Ex. 48

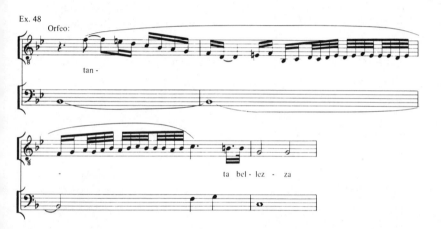

The survival of only the Lament from *Arianna* (xi, 161)[7] has given rise to doubts concerning Monteverdi's authorship of the complete opera.[8] But his claim to have set 1,500 lines of poetry for the festivities of 1608 cannot be much of an exaggeration, since the 1,115 lines of *Arianna,* with about 300 for *Il Ballo delle Ingrate* and *L'Idropica,* do not fall far short of his estimated figure. In addition to the complete set of material for the Mantuan performance, there was a score copied for

7. Compare the manuscript version in Florence, Biblioteca nazionale, transcribed as an appendix to Vogel, *Claudio Monteverdi,* p. 443.
8. Canal, *Della musica in Mantova,* p. 112.

Franceso de' Medici in 1613,[9] and another copied for Striggio in 1620.[10] This version was apparently an improved one, and doubtless further changes were made for the revival in 1639, when *Arianna* opened the season at the Teatro di San Moisè in Venice. It is difficult to believe that so many scores and sets of parts have been lost, almost without trace, even though the imperial troops wrought havoc in Mantua in 1630.

The Lament is a jewel, however, and both Monteverdi and G. B. Doni tell us that it should be regarded as the most essential part of the opera.[11] Its premiere did not take place until considerable effort had been expanded in such matters as the search for good instrumentalists,[12] and the ceaseless casting about for competent singers.[13] Even then, the tragic death of the young soprano Caterina Martinelli cast a long shadow over the production, which was saved only by the last-minute substitution of the actress-singer Virginia Andreini.[14] The poet Marini recalled her moving interpretation of Ariadne in canto 7 of his *Adone*; and when Adriana Basile sang the role in Naples — so beautifully that Theseus himself would have relented — the Duke of Laurenzana immortalized the occasion in verse.[15]

Since no less than fifteen of Monteverdi's letters provide detailed discussion of *La finta pazza Licori,* the

---

9. Davari, *Notizie biografiche*, p. 123. The manuscript of the Lament in Florence may possibly have been part of this copy.

10. Letters of March 17, 20, 28; April 4, 18; May 10.

11. Letter of March 20, 1620. See also Doni, *Lyra Barberina*, 1:124; 2:25,65,80; App. pp. 26, 98.

12. Letter of Carlo Rossi, March 14, 1608, cited by Canal, *Della musica in Mantova,* p. 91.

13. Rinuccini to Striggio, December 20, 1607, cited by Davari, *Notizie biografiche*, p. 88. Grand Duke of Tuscany to Vincenzo Gonzaga, December 4, 1607, Davari, *Notizie biografiche*, p. 89.

14. Davari, *Notizie biografiche*, p. 90.

15. Ademollo, *La bell' Adriana*, p. 14.

first of his two operas on texts by Giulio Strozzi, the total disappearance of this work is doubly unfortunate, for it was probably the first comic opera ever composed. The libretto, written expressly for a soirée at the palazzo Mocenigo, underwent considerable changes in the interests of satisfying and accommodating Monteverdi's musical ideas. Strozzi was neither the first nor the last poet to bend his muse to the dictates of an unusually strong-minded composer, but he survived the ordeal to collaborate yet again with Monteverdi in *Proserpina rapita,* for the marriage festivities of Mocenigo's daughter Giustiniana and Lorenzo Giustiniani in 1630.[16] The music for this opera, the last written by Monteverdi for a private occasion, disappeared completely except for the "Canzonetta Parthenia," *Come dolce oggi l'auretta spira,* "sung by three nymphs in Lydian harmony; that is, with a soft sound," which is preserved in the *Ninth Book of Madrigals,* published in 1651.

The autumn season of 1639 saw the production of *Adone* (on a libretto by Paolo Vendramin) at the Teatro SS. Giovanni e Paolo, so that, with *Arianna* at San Moisè a few months later, it was possible to attend an early and a late opera by Monteverdi in one and the same season. A comparable opportunity presented itself in the following year, when the composer launched yet another new work — *Il Ritorno d'Ulisse in Patria* (xii).[17] Formerly, but

16. The date of the marriage is given as 1629 in Pompeo Litta, *Celebri famiglie italiane*, Series I, Dispensa 157 (Milan, 1868).
17. First edited in modern times by R. Haas, *Denkmäler der Tonkunst in Österreich* 29, Vol. 57, (1922). The most recent and thorough studies of this opera are by W. Osthoff — "Zu den Quellen von Monteverdi's 'Ritorno d'Ulisse in Patria'," *Studien zur Musikwissenschaft* 23 (1956):67; "Zur Bolognese Aufführung von Monteverdis 'Ritorno di Ulisse' im Jahre 1640," *Anzeiger der phil.-hist. Klasse der Osterreichischen Akademie der Wissenschaften* 8 (1958):155; *Das dramatische Spätwerk Claudio Monteverdis* (Tutzing, 1960). For a detailed study of textual problems, see A. Chiarelli, " 'L'Incoronazione di Poppea' o 'Il Nerone': problemi di filologia testuale," *Rivista Italiana di Musicologia* 9 (1974):117.

mistakenly, associated with productions in Bologna in 1630 and Venice in 1641, this opera has now been definitively assigned to the season of 1640. To add to the confusion, its authenticity long remained in doubt, principally because the only musical source did not seem to agree with Giacomo Badoaro's libretto,[18] which exists in seven different (and differing) manuscript copies. But there was also a challenge on purely artistic grounds, no less a scholar than Benvenuti coming to the conclusion that the quality of the music fell short of Monteverdi's greatness.[19] These doubts were cast aside with the discovery, by Wolfgang Osthoff, of a letter from Badoaro to Monteverdi in which the question of collaboration is made perfectly clear.[20]

Although a few choruses, notably those of the Nereids and Sirens, the Naiads, and the Moors, were not copied into the surviving score, *Ulisse* is complete enough to afford countless proofs of Monteverdi's genius. The duets so reminiscent of Book VII ("De' nostri amor concordi" —xii, 29), the trios akin to those of Book IX ("Ama dunque, si si"—xii, 107), and the battle symphony sounding so much like the comparable pieces of Book VIII (xii, 167) all rank as quintessentially Claudian; to which the fine arioso of Penelope ("Torna il tranquillo al mare" —xii, 20) surely deserves to be added, especially in view of its plaintive chromatic ascent:

18. Vogel, "Claudio Monteverdi," p. 403. See especially section D of Osthoff's *Das dramatische Spätwerk.* . . .
19. " 'Il ritorno d'Ulisse in patria' non è di Claudio Monteverdi," *Il Gazzettino* (Venice), May 17, 1942, p. 3.
20. Osthoff, "Zu den Quellen," p. 73.

Ex. 49

Penelope:

tu sol___ del tuo tor - nar, del tuo tor - nar. tu

sol___ del tuo tor - nar per - des - tíil gior - no.

If *Le nozze d'Enea con Lavinia*[21] is lost, there should be
rejoicing over the survival of *L'Incoronazione di Poppea*
(xiii),[22] for which we have two considerably divergent
copies of a lost autograph and at least seven copies of the
libretto by G. F. Busenello.[23] Of the libretti, one
preserved at Treviso agrees most closely with what must
have been the original version performed in 1642 at the
Teatro SS. Giovanni e Paolo. Once again the orchestral
forces are modest,[24] and the choral participation is
minimal. The plot, based for the first time on a historical
theme, gave Monteverdi the chance he had long waited
for; he was finally able to show in his music the develop-
ments and changes in character as one might have
observed them in humans, not gods. He rose to meet the
challenge with every device, every subtlety in his artistic
armory. Ground basses, balanced forms, key schemes,
arioso-recitatives, vocal embellishments, contrasting
ritornels — these and many more are deployed with all the

21. Also based on a libretto by Badoaro.
22. A new critical edition by Alan Curtis is due to appear shortly.
23. See Osthoff, *Das dramatische Spätwerk*, sec. C.
24. See Janet E. Beat, "Monteverdi and the Opera Orchestra of his Time," *The
Monteverdi Companion*, p. 277.

art of a mature musician intent on raising the opera to a
new level of emotional experience. Nero and Poppea,
each a treasure to the other, sing the most beautiful of all
Monteverdi's duets in the sure knowledge that his music
itself is the treasure, shining brilliantly through no matter
what arrangement, orchestration, or adaptation might
be foisted upon it.

Ex. 50

# Selected Bibliography

Abert, Anna Amalie, *Claudio Monteverdi und das musikalische Drama.* Lippstadt, 1954.

Ademollo, Alessandro, *La bella Adriana.* Città di Castello, 1888.

Aldrich, Putnam. *Rhythm in Seventeenth-Century Italian Monody.* New York, 1966.

Antonicek, Theophil, "Claudio Monteverdi und Oesterreich," Oesterreichische Musikzeitschrift 26 (1971): 267.

Arnold, Denis, *Claudio Monteverdi.* London, 1963.

_____. "Formal Design in Monteverdi's Church Music," in *Claudio Monteverdi e il suo tempo.* Verona, 1969.

Barassi, Elena Ferrari, "Il madrigale spirituale nel cinquecento e la raccolta monteverdiana del 1583," in *Claudio Monteverdi e il suo tempo.* Verona, 1969.

Beat, Janet E. "Monteverdi and the Opera Orchestra of His Time" in *The Monteverdi Companion.* London, 1968.

Bertolotti, Antonio, *Musici alla corte dei Gonzaga in Mantova del sec. XV al XVIII.* Milan, 1890.

Biella, Giuseppe, "I Vespri dei Santi di Claudio Monteverdi," *Musica Sacra* 90 (1966): 144.

Bonta, Stephen, "Liturgical Problems in Monteverdi's Marian Vespers," *Journal of the American Musicological Society* 20 (1967): 87.

Brindle, Reginald Smith, "Monteverdi's G minor Mass: an Experiment in Construction," *The Musical Quarterly* 54 (1968): 352.

Canal, Pietro, *Della musica in Mantova*. Venice, 1881.

Cavicchi, Adriano, "Teatro monteverdiano e tradizione teatrale ferrarese," in *Claudio Monteverdi e il suo tempo*. Verona, 1969.

Davari, Stefano, *Notizie biografiche del distinto maestro di musica Claudio Monteverdi*. Mantua, 1885.

Doni, Giovanni Battista, *Lyra Barberina*. Florence, 1763.

Donington, Robert, "Monteverdi's First Opera," in *The Monteverdi Companion*. London, 1968.

Einstein, Alfred, "Abbot Angelo Grillo's Letters as Source Material for Music History," in *Essays on Music*. New York, 1956.

Errante, Vincenzo. "Forse che sì, forse che no." *Archivio Storico Lombardo* 42, ser. 5 (1915): 31.

Federhofer, Hellmut. "Graz Court Musicians and their contributions to the *Parnassus Musicus Ferdinandaeus* (1615)." *Musica Disciplina* 9 (1955): 167.

Frati, Lodovico. "Il Petrarca e la musica." *Rivista musicale italiana* 31 (1924): 59.

Gallico, Claudio. "La 'Lettera amorosa' di Monteverdi." *Nuova rivista musicale italiana* 1 (1967): 287.

Jeppesen, Knud. "Monteverdi, Kappelmeister am S.ta Barbara?", in *Claudio Monteverdi e il suo tempo*. Verona, 1969.

Lavin, Irving. "Lettres de Parme (1618, 1627-28) et débuts du théâtre baroque," in *Le Lieu théâtral à la Renaissance*. Paris, 1969.

Litta, Pompeo. *Celebri famiglie italiane* 157, ser. 1. Milan, 1868.

Lupo, Bettina. "Sacre monodie monteverdiane." *Musica* 2 (1943): 70.

MacClintock, Carol. *Giaches de Wert*. Rome, 1966.

————. "New Sources of Mantuan Music." *Journal of the American Musicological Society* 22 (1969): 508.

Nagler, A. M. *Theatre Festivals of the Medici, 1539-1637*. New Haven, Conn., 1964.

Osthoff, Wolfgang. *Das dramatische Spätwerk Claudio Monteverdis*. Tutzing, 1960.

————. "Zu den Quellen von Monteverdis 'Ritorno d'Ulisse in Patria'." *Studien zur Musikwissenschaft* 23 (1956): 67.

————. "Monteverdi-Funde." *Archiv für Musikwissenschaft* 14 (1957): 253.

————. "Zur Bologneser Aufführung von Monteverdis 'Ritorno d'Ulisse' im Jahre 1640." *Anzeiger der phil.-hist. Klasse der Oesterreichischen Akademie der Wissenschaften* 8 (1958): 155.

————. "Monteverdis *Combattimento* in deutscher Sprache und Heinrich Schütz," in *Festschrift Helmuth Osthoff zum 65. Geburtstage*. Tutzing, 1961.

_____. "Unità liturgica e artistica." *Rivista italiana di musicologia* 2 (1967): 314.

Paoli, Domenico de. *Claudio Monteverdi*. Milan, 1945.

_____. *Claudio Monteverdi: Lettere, dediche, prefazioni*. Rome, 1973.

Pirrotta, Nino. *Scelte poetiche di Monteverdi*. Rome, 1968.

Prunières, Henry. *Monteverdi*. New York, 1926.

Redlich, Hans. *Claudio Monteverdi*. London, 1952.

Reiner, Stuart. "Preparations in Parma—1618, 1627-28." *The Music Review* 25 (1964): 273.

Roche, Jerome. "Monteverdi—An Interesting Example of Second Thoughts." *The Music Review* 32 (1971): 193.

Sansovino, Francesco. *Venetia città nobilissima*. Venice, 1663.

Santoro, Elia. *Iconografia Monteverdiana*. Cremona, 1968.

Schrade, Leo. *Monteverdi: Creator of Modern Music*. London, 1951.

Solerti, Angelo. *Gli albori del melodramma*. Milan, 1905.

_____. *Musica, ballo, e drammatica all corte Medicea dal 1600 al 1637*. Florence, 1905.

_____. "Un balletto musicato da Claudio Monteverdi." *Rivista musicale italiana* 11 (1904): 24.

Stevens, Denis. "Where are the Vespers of Yesteryear?." *The Musical Quarterly* 47 (1961): 315.

_____. "Madrigali Guerrieri, et Amorosi." *The Musical Quarterly* 53 (1967): 161.

_____. "Claudio Monteverdi: *Selva morale e spirituale*," in *Claudio Monteverdi e il suo tempo*. Verona, 1969.

_____. "Wagner vs. Monteverdi." *American Choral Review* 12 (1970): 95.

_____. "Monteverdi's Necklace." *The Musical Quarterly* 59 (1973): 370.

Strunk, Oliver. *Source Readings in Music History*. New York, 1950.

Tagmann, Pierre. *Archivalische Studien zur Musikpflege am Dom von Mantua (1500-1627)*. Bern and Stuttgart, 1967.

Vecchi, Giuseppi. *Le Accademie Musicali del primo seicento e Monteverdi a Bologna*. Bologna, 1969.

Vogel, Emil. "Claudio Monteverdi." *Vierteljahrsschrift für Musikwissenschaft* 3 (1887): 430.

Watkins, Glenn. *Carlo Gesualdo*. London, 1973.

Willetts, Pamela J. "A Neglected Source of Monody and Madrigal." *Music and Letters* 43 (1962): 329.

# Index

Abert, Anna Amalie, 118n
Accademici Intrepidi (Ferrara), 16
Achillini, Claudio, 111, 127, 128
Ademollo, Alessandro, 116n,117n, 134n
Agnelli, Scipione, 35, 125
Alberti, Filippo, 27
Aldrich, Putnam, 114n
Allegretti, Antonio, 27,n
Ambrosini, Pietro, 16, 44
Andreini, Giovan Battista, 111
Andreini, Virginia, 111,119,134
Anselmi, Giovanni Battista, 48, 55
Antonicek, Theophil, 99n
Arlotti, Ridolfo, 32
Arnold, Denis, 70n, 99n, 100n, 101n
Atanagi, Dionigi, 27n
    De le Rime di diversi nobili poeti
    toscani, I (1565), 27n
Atti, Francesco degli, 53n

Badoaro, Giacomo, 136, 137n
Barassi, Elena Ferrari, 16n
Baranardi, Dom Odoardo, 66
Barblan, Guglielmo, 114n
Basile, Adriana, 57n, 58, 59, 60, 62, 126, 134
Basile, Margherita, 58
Beat, Janet E., 137n
Belli, Girolamo, 27
Bembo, Giovanni Mateo, 35n
Bembo, Pietro, 27, 37

Bentivoglio, Enzo, 116n, 127
Bentivoglio, Ercole, 27
Benvenuti, Giacomo, 136
Berchem, Jachet van, 68n
Bertolotti, Antonio, 116n, 132n
Bianchi, Giulio Cesare, 100, 101
Bianco, Pietro, 27n
Boethius, 112
Bonometti, Giovanni Battista, 99;
    Parnassus Musicus Ferdinandaeus,99
Bonta, Stephen, 74n
Bovicelli, Giovanni Battista, 75
Brindle, Reginald Smith, 72n
Brunelli, Antonio, 114n
Busenello, Gian Francesco, 137
Buttigli, Marcello, 128

Caccini, Settimia, 128
Cagnani, Eugenio, 131n
Calvo, Lorenzo, 101;
    Symbolae diversorum musicorum, 101
Camarella, Giovanni Battista, 61
Campagnolo, Francesco, 58, 59
Canal, Pietro, 118n, 133n, 134n
Caninio, Dom Stefano, 66, 98
Capello, Pietro, 16
Carretto, Agnese del, 110
Carretto, Silvio del, 110
Carver, Robert, 101n
Casati, Gasparo, 103
Casola, Don Bassano, 67

Casoni, Girolamo, 27
Cavicchi, Adriano, 110n
Cesana, Bartolomeo, 53n
Chiabrera, Gabriello, 47, 125
Conforto, Giovanni Luca, 75
Cooper, Kenneth, 120n
Coppini, Aquilino, 36n, 66, 98;
  *Musica tolta da i madrigali di
  Claudio Monteverdi, 99*
Coryate, Thomas, 101
Crotti, Arcangelo, 99n
Curtis, Alan, 137n

D'Accone, Frank, 79n
Davari, Stefano, 126n, 134n
Doni, Giovanni Battista, 35, 111,
  117n, 134
Donington, Robert, 131n
Dunstable, John, 95n

Einstein, Alfred, 59n
Errante, Vincenzo, 73n
Este, Cesare I, Duke of Modena, 45

Fairfax, Edward, 31n
Farnese, Odoardo, Duke of Parma,
  122, 127
Federhofer, Hellmut, 53n, 99n
Fei, Michel'Angelo, 16n
Ferdinand, Archduke (later
  Ferdinand II, Holy Roman
  Emperor), 53n, 99, 126
Ferdinand III, Holy Roman Emperor,
  16, 40, 50, 121
Ferrari, Cherubino, 132
Follino, Federico, 125
Fraganesco, Alessandro, 16
Franzoni, Amante, 99n
Frati, Lodovico, 38n, 45n
Funghetti, Paolo, 16n

Gabrieli, Andrea, 23
Gabrieli, Giovanni, 101n
Gagliano, Marco da, 131;
  *Dafne*, 131
Gallico, Claudio, 75n, 111n
Gastoldi, Gian Giacomo, 29n
Gesualdo, Carlo, Principe di Venosa,
  27, 29, 32
Gigli, Giulio, 27n;
  *Sdegnosi ardori*, 27n
Giustiniani, Lorenzo, 37, 135

Gombert, Nicholas, 68, 68n;
  *In illo tempore*, 67
Gonzaga, Caterina Medici, Duchess of
  Mantua, 16, 111
Gonzaga, Eleonora (later Empress
  Eleonora), 66, 118, 126
Gonzaga, Ferdinando, Sixth Duke of
  Mantua, 45, 67n, 116n, 125
Gonzaga, Francesco, Fifth Duke of
  Mantua, 16, 48, 49n, 118, 132
Gonzaga, Vincenzo, Fourth Duke of
  Mantua, 16, 34, 101, 110, 116, 118,
  134n
Gonzaga, Vincenzo II, Seventh Duke of
  Mantua, 49n
Goretti, Antonio, 127
Grillo, Angelo, 35n, 57n, 59
Gualberto, Giovanni, 131
Guarini, Giambattista, 19, 23, 27, 29,
  31, 36, 38, 53, 54, 57n, 60, 110;
  *Il pastor fido*, 19, 31, 33, 54;
  *L'Idropica*, 124, 133
Guerrero, Francisco, 79n
Guitti, Francesco, 127

Haas, Robert, 135n
Harràn, Don, 21n
Henry IV, King of France, 49-50

Iberti, Annibale, 120n
Ingegneri, Angelo, 19, 27n
Inghirami, Luigi, 128

Jeppesen, Knud, 83n

Kroyer, Theodor, 21n

Lappi, Pietro, 66, 99n
Laurenzana, Duke of, 57n, 134
Lavin, Irving, 127n
Litta, Pompeo, 135n
Lupo, Bettina, 95
Luzzaschi, Luzzasco, 19n

MacClintock, Carol, 16n, 19n
McKelvy, James, 81n
Magni, Bartolomeo, 55
Marenzio, Luca, 23n, 55n
Margherita of Savoy (later Duchess of
  Mantua), 118
Marigliani, Ercole, 126
Marini, Giambattista, 23, 36, 37, 38,
  59, 134

Marinoni, Giovanni Battista, 103
Martinelli, Caterina, 33, 134
Masnelli, Paolo, 27
Matthaei, Karl, 74n
Mazzi, Francesco, 127
Medici, Cosimo II, Grand Duke of
  Tuscany, 69
Medici, Ferdinando I, Grand Duke of
  Tuscany, 134n
Medici, Ferdinando II, Grand Duke of
  Tuscany, 37
Medici, Francesco de', 134
Medici, Gian Carlo de', 128
Medici, Margherita de', 127
Milanuzzi, Carlo, 60
Mocenigo, Girolamo, 37, 135
Mocenigo, Giustiniana, 135
Monteverdi, Claudia, 23, 33
Monteverdi, Claudio, passim. Works:
  *A Dio, Florida bella,* 23, 34
  *A quest' olmo,* 37
  *A un giro sol,* 31
  *Ab aeterno ordinata sum,* 103
  *Adone,* 131, 134, 135
  *Adoramus te, Christe,* 101
  *Ah, dolente partita,* 19
  *Ahi, che si parti,* 46
  *Ahi, come a un vago sol,* 22, 23n
  *Al lume delle stelle,* 37
  *Alcun non mi consigli,* 51
  *Altri canti d'Amor,* 38, 40
  *Altri canti di Marte,* 38
  *Aminta, Prologue and Intermezzi,* 127
  *Amor, che deggio far,* 37
  *Andromeda,* 108
  *Anima mia* [Deh, Mirtillo), 19
  *Apollo, Lament of,* 35n, 112
  *Ardo avvampo,* 38, 40
  *Ardo, e scoprir,* 38
  *Ardo, si, ma non t'amo,* 27
  *Arianna,* 130, 133, 134, 135
  *Armato il cor,* 38, 55, 56
  *Armida,* 114
  *Audi coelum,* 99
  *Ave maris stella,* 74, 79

  *Baci soave e cari,* 27

  *Ballo, Movete al mio bel suon,* 38, 121
  *Batto qui pianse,* 34
  *Beatus vir I* (1641), 84, 88, 89
  *Beatus vir II* (1641), 84
  *Bel pastor,* 25

  *Cantate Domino* (1615), 99
  *Cantate Domino* (1620), 100
  *Ch'io ami la vita mia,* 27
  *Chiome d'oro,* 54, 88
  *Ch'io t'ami,* 19, 20
  *Chi vuol haver felice,* 36, 38, 88
  *Chi vuol veder,* 45
  *Christe adoramus te,* 101
  *Combattimento di Tancredi e Clorinda,*
    38, 40, 109, 112, 113, 114
  *Come dolce oggi,* 51, 135
  *Con che soavita,* 59, 60
  *Confitebor I* (1641), 84
  *Confitebor II* (1641), 84
  *Confitebor III* (1641), 36n, 84n, 87
  *Confitebor I* (1650), 86
  *Confitebor II* (1650), 86
  *Credo a 7,* 70, 85
  *Cruda Amarilli,* 19
  *Crudel, perchè mi fuggi,* 29
  *Currite populi,* 102

  *De la bellezza,* 117
  *Deus tuorum militum,* 90
  *Dice la mia bellissima Clori,* 54
  *Dixit Dominus* (1610), 74
  *Dixit Dominus I* (1641), 84, 86, 87
  *Dixit Dominus II* (1641), 84
  *Dixit Dominus I* (1650), 79, 86, 87
  *Dixit Dominus II* (1650), 79, 80
  *Dolcissimo uscignuolo,* 36, 38, 88
  *Domine ad adjuvandum,* 74

  *Ecce sacrum paratum,* 102
  *Ecco di dolci raggi,* 61
  *Ecco mormorar l'onde,* 29, 100
  *Ecco Silvio,* 19

E così a poco a poco, 23
Ed è pur dunque vero, 61
Ego dormio, 102
Endimione, 117
En gratulemur hodie, 91
Exulta filia, 102
Exultent caeli, 102

Filli cara e amata, 27
Fugge anima mea, 101
Fumia la pastorella, 27

Gira il nemico, 38, 50
Gloria a 7, 69n, 70
Gloria a 8, 69

Hor, care canzonette, 44
Hor che 'l ciel, 38, 40

I cinque fratelli, 37
Iam moriar, 103
Il Ballo delle Ingrate, 38, 118, 133
Il Pastor Fido, 19, 31, 33, 110
Il Ritorno d'Ulisse, 131, 135, 136
Incenerite spoglie (see Lagrime d'Amante)
Intermezzi for Aminta, 127
Intermezzi for Le Tre Constanti, 126
Intermezzi for Mercurio e Marte, 127, 128
Interrotte speranze, 54
Io mi son giovinetta, 21
Iste confessor, 90

Jubilet tota civitas, 103.

Laetatus sum (1610), 74, 77, 81
Laetatus sum I (1650), 81
Laetatus sum II (1650), 80
La finta pazza Licori, 130, 134
Lagrime d'Amante, 35
La Maddalena, 111
Lamento della Ninfa, 25, 38, 114
Lamento d'Olimpia, 61

La mia turca, 60
Lapidabant Stephanum, 98
Lasciatemi morire, 34, 35, 103
Lauda Jerusalem (1610), 74, 78
Lauda Jerusalem I (1650), 81
Lauda Jerusalem II (1650), 80
Laudate Dominum (Ps. 116) I (1641), 84n, 89
Laudate Dominum (Ps. 116) II (1641), 84
Laudate Dominum (Ps. 116) III (1641), 84
Laudate Dominum (Ps. 116) (1650), 103
Laudate Dominum (Ps. 150), 103
Laudate pueri (1610), 74, 77
Laudate pueri I (1641), 84
Laudate pueri II (1641), 84
Laudate pueri (1650), 80
La Vittoria d'Amore, 122
Le Nozze d'Enea con Lavinia, 131, 137
Le Nozze di Tetide, 125, 126
Le Tre Costanti, 126
Lettera amorosa, 111
L'Incoronazione di Poppea, 130, 131, 137, 138
Litany of the B.V.M., 101
Luci serene e chiare, 32

Magnificat a 6 (1610), 74, 79
Magnificat a 7 (1610), 74, 79
Magnificat I (1641), 84, 85, 92
Magnificat II (1641), 84, 91
Mentre vaga Angioletta, 38, 56
M'è più dolce, 19
Mercurio e Marte, 127, 128
Messa Salmi, Letanie (1650), 79
Misero Alceo, 23, 24, 34
Missa In illo tempore, 68
Missa a 4 (1641), 70
Missa a 4 (1650), 72
Movete al mio bel suon, 38, 121

Ninfa che scalza, 38
Nisi Dominus (1610), 74, 77
Nisi Dominus I (1650), 81
Nisi Dominus II (1650), 80
Non è di gentil core, 53

[145]

Non partir ritrosetta, 38
Non si levava ancor, 27
Non voglio amare, 51

O beatàe viae, 101
O bone Jesu, 101
O ciechi, 42
O come gran martire, 29
O come vaghi, 55
Ogni amante è guerrier, 38, 49
Ohimè, ch'io cado, 60, 61
Ohimè, dove é mio ben, 55
Ohimè, il bel viso, 34
O Mirtillo, 19
O primavera, 19n
Orfeo, 47, 48, 74, 99, 130, 131, 132
O sia tranquillo il mar, 38, 56

Partenza amorosa, 111
Perchè mi fuggi, 38
Perchè, se m'odiavi, 51
Piagne e sospira, 32
Più lieto il guardo, 61
Presso un fiume tranquillo, 24, 34
Proserpina rapita, 51, 130, 135
Prologue, L'Aminta, 127
Prologue, La Maddalena, 111
Prologue, L'Idropica, 125

Qual si può dir, 44
Quando dentro al tuo seno, 51
Quell' augellin, 19
Quel sguardo sdegnosetto, 61
Questi vaghi concenti, 23
Qui rise, O Tirsi, 37

Rosaio Fiorito, 17n

Sacrae Cantiunculae, 98
Salve Regina I (1641), 94
Salve Regina II (1641), 96
Salve Regina III (1641), 96
Salve Regina IV (1624), 97
Salve Regina V (1625), 97
Sancta Maria, succurre, 102

Sanctorum meritis, 90
Scherzi Musicali (1607), 47, 48, 50, 53, 117, 125
Scherzi Musicali (1632), 55, 60
Selva Morale e Spirituale, 26n, 36, 40, 42, 43n, 50, 70, 79, 83, 85, 95, 103
Se vittorie si belle, 38
Sfogava con le stelle, 32
Sì, ch'io vorrei morrire, 32
Sì dolce è il tormento, 60
Sonata sopra Sancta Maria, 99
Su su su, pastorelli, 38, 50

Taci Armelin, 48, 55
T'amo, mia vita, 22
Tempro la cetra, 59
Tirsi e Clori, 24, 117, 120, 121
Tropo ben può questo tiranno, 22

Una donna fra l'altra, 34, 36
Ut queant laxis, 90

Vaghi rai, 47
Vago augelletto, 38
Vattene pur, crudel, 31
Venite sitientes, 101
Vivrò fra i miei tormenti, 30
Voglio di vita uscir, 61
Voi ch'ascoltate, 42

Zefiro torna (Rinuccini), 55, 61
Zefiro torna (Petrarch), 34
Monteverdi, Francesco, 69, 69n
Monteverdi, Giulio Cesare, 49n, 117, 132
Morandi, Bernardo, 122
Moro, Maurizio, 32
Morsolino, Antonio, 45
Mouton, Jean, 68n

Nagler, A. M., 127n, 128n

Orlandi, Sante, 132
Orologio, Gerolamo, 16
Osthoff, Wolfgang, 45n, 61n, 69n, 74n, 102n, 113n, 135n, 136, 137n

[146]

Palestrina, Giovanni Pierluigi da, 101n
Paoli, Domenico de, 51n, 61n
Parma, Alberto, 27
Paul V, Pope, 66, 67
Peri Jacopo, 131;
    *Euridice*, 131
Petrarch, 33, 37, 38, 40, 43n, 45, 55n
    *Trionfo della morte*, 42
Pio, Ascanio, 127
Pirrotta, Nino, 32n, 43n, 45n, 50n,
    114n, 121n
Plato, 112, 125
Ponzio, Pietro, 16n
Porter, Walter, 33
Praetorius, Hieronymus, 88n
Profe, Ambrosius, 66
Prunières, Henry, 46n

Rasi, Francesco, 58, 131
Redlich, Hans Ferdinand, 68n
Reiner, Stuart, 127n
Ricardi, Giacomo, 16
Rinuccini, Ottavio, 25, 32, 38, 49,
    55, 134n
Roche, Jerome, 86n
Rossi, Carlo, 134n
Ruuli, Rinaldo, 16n

Sacrati, Francesco, 135
Salinis, Hubertus de, 95
Sammaruco, Francesco, 101;
    *Sacri affetti*, 101
Sances, Felice, 69n
Santoro, Elia, 49n
Schrade, Leo, 98n
Schütz, Heinrich, 19n, 113
Sirena, Galeazzo, 107
Solerti, Angelo, 122n, 125n, 126n,
    127n
Sordi, Camillo, 120n
Steele, John, 70n

Stevens, Denis, 21n, 34n, 40n, 101n,
    103n
Stevenson, Robert, 79n
Striggio, Alessandro, 58, 69n, 107,
    118, 120n, 125, 127, 132, 133, 134
Strom, Reinhart, 59n
Strozzi, Giulio, 51, 135;
    *I cinque fratelli*, 37;
    *La finta pazza Licori*, 134;
    *Proserpina rapita*, 51, 130, 135
Strunk, Oliver, 112n
Susato, Tielman, 68n

Tagmann, Pierre, 83n
Tasso, Bernardo, 55
Tasso, Torquato, 27, 29, 32, 37;
    *Aminta*, 127;
    *Gerusalemme conquistata*, 32;
    *Gerusalemme liberata*, 30, 112, 113
Testi, Fulvio, 57n

Vendramin, Paolo, 135;
    *Adone*, 135
Verità, Count Marco, 16, 27
Viadana, Lodovico Grossi da, 75n;
    *Cento concerti ecclesiastici*, 75
Vogel, Emil, 17n, 69n, 70n, 133n,
    136n

Walker, Daniel Pickering, 107n
Walker, Frank, 127n
Watkins, Glenn, 32n
Watson, Thomas, 29n, 55n
Wert, Giaches de, 19n, 68, 68n;
    *Missa Transeunte Domino*, 68
Willaert, Adrian, 23
Willetts, Pamela, 33

Yonge, Nicholas, 29n

Zuccari, Federico, 117

[147]